"In her warm, accessible style, Eileen Kennedy[...] [...]ventional thinking about self-esteem on its he[...] parents, and to anyone who works with or ca[...] Confidence makes a compelling argument [...] frantic attempts to pump up our children [...] Kennedy-Moore lays out a plan to address the need for connection, competence, and choice—three critical factors at the heart of a 'quiet ego.' It is possible to dive into any one chapter and emerge armed with practical suggestions. Better yet, read the whole book. This one is a game-changer."

> —**Dawn Huebner, PhD**, psychologist, parent coach,
> and author of *Outsmarting Worry*

"*Kid Confidence* is packed with surprising and realistic advice about how we can help kids stop worrying about if they are *good enough*. In her uniquely wonderful way, Kennedy-Moore also gives us the confidence to handle any parenting challenge."

> —**Diane Debrovner,** deputy editor at *Parents* magazine

"The best parenting resource I have seen in several years. Too many children and teens suffer from a negative inward focus on themselves that is self-critical and self-judgmental. Outwardly, they may seem anxious or depressed, worried or discouraged. Child and family psychologist Eileen Kennedy-Moore shows parents the road to helping children develop real self-esteem and 'a quiet ego' through connection, competence, and choice. The book is firmly evidence-based, developmentally based, practically based, and it is fundamentally wise and compassionate."

> —**Carol D. Goodheart, EdD**, former president of
> the American Psychological Association

"Not just another parenting book! Eileen Kennedy-Moore relies on solid research to reveal why much of what we've been taught about raising self-confident children is actually counterproductive. *Kid Confidence* offers a wealth of wisdom and practical strategies aimed at helping parents succeed at instilling their children with authentic self-esteem through reducing self-focus and harsh self-judgment."

—**Mary K. Alvord, PhD**, psychologist, and coauthor
of *Conquer Negative Thinking for Teens* and *Resilience Builder Program for Children and Adolescents*

"An exciting alternative to most books about self-esteem. Eileen Kennedy-Moore helps parents boost their child's skills in the critical areas of making friends, making choices, and mastering the ups and downs of the learning process. Every parent, grandparent, and school counselor can benefit from the specific tips and guidance in this book. Wise, compassionate, and grounded in the latest research, *Kid Confidence* delivers on its promise to help children develop authentic confidence."

—**Meg Selig, NCC**, a retired counselor,
and author of *Changepower!*

"Traditional approaches to building self-esteem and confidence often encourage a rather egoic approach that can inadvertently make children more self-focused, insecure, and unhappy. Drawing on the latest theory and research in psychology, Eileen Kennedy-Moore offers insights and advice by which parents can foster their children's well-being by promoting their social connections, competence, and feelings of choice and control. Not only are these the pillars of happiness and lifelong well-being, but when parents focus on these important considerations, self-esteem and self-confidence take care of themselves."

—**Mark R. Leary, PhD**, Garonzik Family Professor
of Psychology and Neuroscience at Duke University,
and author of *The Curse of the Self*

"In this enlightening and refreshing book, Eileen Kennedy-Moore puts forth the premise that we can't just 'teach' our kids to have self-confidence, but rather that we grow it with them through our relationships. Parents and teachers alike will benefit from the book's powerful message that our connection with our kids is the foundation of self-esteem."

—**Mona Delahooke, PhD,** clinical psychologist,
and author *of Social and Emotional Development in Early Intervention*

"What child couldn't use some help through the rocky road of childhood? Be it making friends, making good decisions, or having a can-do attitude, Eileen Kennedy-Moore skillfully guides parents in how to help children develop authentic self-esteem, and build their resilience to meet the inevitable rough patches and pressures of growing up today. *Kid Confidence* provides vital understanding and strategies to cultivate confident kids that parents can confidently send out into the world…with pride."

—**Susan Newman, PhD**, social psychologist,
and author of *Little Things Long Remembered* and
The Book of NO

"*Kid Confidence* is a must-read parenting book! Eileen offers keen insight into how to ease a child's harsh self-focus, which is the foundation for raising an emotionally healthy child."

—**Maureen Healy**, author of *The Emotionally Healthy Child*

"*Kid Confidence* is essential reading for those who seek to guide children who experience low self-esteem. Eileen Kennedy-Moore emphasizes the importance of connection, competence, and choice. She conveys a wealth of understandings, and shares practical strategies designed to help children temper tendencies toward harsh or negative self-focus. For example, she discusses how to forge meaningful relationships, maximize effort, recognize unproductive rumination, build decision-making skills, and develop the confidence and joy of a quiet ego. Kennedy-Moore reveals myriad ways kids can embrace a kinder, realistic, more empowered sense of self."

> —**Joanne Foster, EdD**, educational consultant, and
> award-winning author of five books on child
> development, giftedness, and productivity—
> including *Beyond Intelligence*; *Not Now, Maybe Later*;
> and *Bust Your BUTS*

"*Kid Confidence* effectively takes on the wrongheaded but popular idea that a child's self-esteem is built on heaps of praise and the absence of criticism, and instead presents clearly articulated strategies to help your child become more resilient, self-reliant, and happy. Eileen Kennedy-Moore casts a wide net, discussing every aspect of a child's life, including relationships with adults, siblings, and friends; learning to manage emotions; and acquiring social skills. Along the way, she highlights the impact predictable problems will have on the development of healthy self-esteem, and how to counter them. Informed by both her clinical experience and the latest psychological research, she has given parents a valuable guidebook to navigating the hard job of raising children well."

> —**Peg Streep,** author of *Daughter Detox* and
> *Mean Mothers*

"In *Kid Confidence*, trusted child development resource Eileen Kennedy-Moore brings to light an important, but often overlooked, truth: Real self-confidence occurs when kids feel connected, competent, and in control, not when parents pour on the praise. Packed with practical, research-based strategies to build resilience and self-esteem, *Kid Confidence* is essential reading for all parents."

—**Katie Hurley, LCSW,** author of *No More Mean Girls*
and *The Happy Kid Handbook*

"*Kid Confidence* is a practical and compassionate guide for any parent seeking to boost a child's self-esteem, grounded in the latest research. Eileen Kennedy-Moore puts to rest the misguided idea that telling kids they're terrific will boost confidence, and instead gives parents effective strategies for building their children's actual capability. The believable dialogue and case studies will help readers strengthen their children's ability to tackle friendship issues, perfectionism, indecision, and low confidence. With youth anxiety and mental illness growing to epidemic levels, Kennedy-Moore has written the book all parents need to read. We need *Kid Confidence* now more than ever."

—**Katherine Reynolds Lewis**, certified parent educator,
and author of *The Good News About Bad Behavior*

KID
CONFIDENCE

**Help Your Child Make Friends,
Build Resilience, *and*
Develop Real Self-Esteem**

EILEEN KENNEDY-MOORE, PhD

New Harbinger Publications, Inc.

Publisher's Note

This publication is designed to provide accurate and authoritative information in regard to the subject matter covered. It is sold with the understanding that the publisher is not engaged in rendering psychological, financial, legal, or other professional services. If expert assistance or counseling is needed, the services of a competent professional should be sought.

Disclaimer: The vignettes in this book are based on composites of children. They are intended to represent typical behavior and problems, and they do not refer to specific people or real events. This book is for general educational purposes only. It does not constitute and should not substitute for psychotherapy or the provision of psychological services.

Distributed in Canada by Raincoast Books

Copyright © 2019 by Eileen Kennedy-Moore
            New Harbinger Publications, Inc.
            5674 Shattuck Avenue
            Oakland, CA 94609
            www.newharbinger.com

Cover design by Amy Shoup

Acquired by Wendy Millstine

Edited by Brady Kahn

All Rights Reserved

Library of Congress Cataloging-in-Publication Data

Names: Kennedy-Moore, Eileen, author.
Title: Kid confidence : help your child make friends, build resilience, and develop real self-esteem / Eileen Kennedy-Moore ; foreword by Michele Borba.
Description: Oakland, CA : New Harbinger Publications, 2019. | Includes bibliographical references.
Identifiers: LCCN 2018031430 (print) | LCCN 2018033638 (ebook) | ISBN 9781684030507 (PDF e-book) | ISBN 9781684030514 (ePub) | ISBN 9781684030491 (paperback)
Subjects: LCSH: Self-esteem in children. | Self-actualization (Psychology) | Interpersonal relations. | Parenting. | BISAC: FAMILY & RELATIONSHIPS / Children with Special Needs. | FAMILY & RELATIONSHIPS / Parenting / General. | SELF-HELP / Personal Growth / Self-Esteem.
Classification: LCC BF723.S3 (ebook) | LCC BF723.S3 K456 2019 (print) | DDC 155.4/182--dc23
LC record available at https://lccn.loc.gov/2018031430

21   20   19

10   9   8   7   6   5   4   3   2   1   First Printing

To my dear friend, Christine McLaughlin.
Thank you for the support, inspiration, and laughter.

Contents

PART 4: Choice

PART 5: The Bigger Picture

Foreword

All parents love their children and want only the best for them. And of course, we do everything and anything in our power to give them what we think they need to achieve success and happiness. It's a big reason why many moms and dads have jumped on the self-esteem bandwagon, insisting their kids be given trophies (even if it's for "showing up"), cushioning them from every bump to protect them from failure, and even urging schools to eliminate red pencils to make sure their children "feel special."

It's not that self-esteem isn't important. The problem is that many times our well-meaning parenting attempts to nurture our kids' confidence and well-being run *counter* to research—and can even reduce our kids' chances for optimum well-being. And it seems our good-intentioned but misaimed parenting has backfired:

- Researchers from Ohio State University[*] surveyed parents and their kids during four periods over one and a half years. They found those who *overvalued* their children (describing them as "more special than other children" and "deserving something extra in life") when the study began ended up with kids who later scored higher on tests of narcissism.

- University of Michigan researchers analyzed over seventy-two studies and found that American teens' narcissism rates increased 58 percent in thirty years while their empathy levels dropped 40 percent.[**]

---

[*] Brummelman, E., et al. 2015. Origins of narcissism in children. PNAS 112 (12); https://doi.org/10.1073/pnas.1420870112.

[**] Konrath, S. H., O'Brien, E. H., and Hsing, C. 2011. Changes in dispositional empathy in American college students over time: A meta-analysis. Personality and Social Psychology Review 15 (2).

These findings are not good news if our hope is to raise confident, caring, competent kids.

So what's a parent to do? Well, you can stop wondering. The answer lies in your hands. *Kid Confidence,* full of research-based and road-tested guidance, holds everything you need to help your child develop both authentic self-esteem and the skills to thrive in today's uncertain world. And it's written by a prominent and trusted parenting expert, Eileen Kennedy-Moore.

I know Eileen and admire her work. She is a practicing clinical psychologist with extensive experience working with adults, children, and families. Eileen is also the author of several acclaimed parenting books, including *Growing Friendships: A Kids' Guide to Making and Keeping Friends; Smart Parenting for Smart Kids;* and *What About Me? 12 Ways to Get Your Parents' Attention (Without Hitting Your Sister).* She regularly speaks at schools and conferences about parenting and child development, and has four children of her own. If anyone can give us a framework to raise confident kids, it's Eileen.

Kid Confidence is a treasure trove of parenting strategies culled from cutting-edge research. Eileen shows you how to instill the *right* kind of self-esteem in your child to reap a brighter future. Here is just a sample of the skills you will learn to help your child build:

- Developing self-calming to prevent big emotional displays

- Encouraging problem-solving to avoid disagreements with peers

- Cultivating friendships by joining in and holding conversations

- Coping with the inevitable schoolyard bullies, teasers, and meanies

- Developing the real self-esteem boosters of grit and stick-to-itiveness

- Cultivating stronger, healthier relationships with siblings

- Making healthy decisions and reducing feelings of help-lessness and indecisiveness

- Reducing the pain of feeling different by learning to fit in to social settings

But that's not all, Eileen offers dozens of practical, proven strategies that guide your child away from the unhealthy self-focus that's the root cause of low self-esteem. "When children are able to fulfill their fundamental needs for connection, competence, and choice, they're less apt to fret about their worth as a human being," Eileen explains. So, she teaches how to cultivate those three crucial C's that cultivate healthy, real self-esteem:

1. *Connection,* to help your child build strong and satisfying relationships;

2. *Competence,* to encourage your child to sustain effort, learn effectively, and let go of unhealthy perfectionism; and

3. *Choice,* to help your child learn to make decisions and figure out personal values.

That's how we will raise confident, resilient, empowered kids.

My only recommendation: use this book! Consistently using the strategies Eileen suggests will help your kids succeed and thrive—not only now, but also for the rest of their lives. And what a difference you'll make!

—Michele Borba, EdD
Author of *UnSelfie: Why Empathetic Kids Succeed in Our All-About-Me World*

PART 1
INTRODUCTION

Why Telling Our Kids They're Wonderful Doesn't Build Real Self-Esteem

...and What Does

"I can't do anything right!"

"Nobody likes me!"

"I'm the worst kid in the world!"

As parents, hearing the children we love make such viciously self-critical comments is heartbreaking. Our first instinct is to rush to contradict them. "That's not true, honey!" we exclaim. Trying to reassure our kids, we quickly marshal example after example of their talent and specialness. Because we love our children so much, it feels intolerable and even unimaginable that they wouldn't love them-selves. But the more we tell our self-doubting kids "You're wonder-ful!" the harder they argue, "I'm terrible!" No matter how sincere and well-meaning our pep talks are, they never seem to sink in when our children are struggling with low self-esteem.

Challenges with self-esteem are very common. Almost every child—and adult—faces moments of self-doubt or periods when they feel inadequate. But for some children, the tendency to view themselves in a negative light is frequent, persistent, and even central to their identity. This book will help you address the root causes of your child's low self-esteem and give you practical strategies to help your child develop real competence and confidence. But first, let's talk about what self-esteem means.

What Is Self-Esteem?

Self-esteem involves evaluations of the self that lead to positive or negative feelings *about* the self. These evaluations reflect how we imagine that other people view us. When kids believe that others think badly of them, they feel bad about themselves.

It's easy to spot low self-esteem in kids: If you've ever said things like, "My son gets so down on himself when he makes a mistake!" or "My daughter gives up before she starts! She's afraid to try," your child may be struggling with low self-esteem. Sometimes low self-esteem is tied to a specific area, such as when a kid believes, "I stink at math!" Other times, it's all-encompassing, as when an older child insists, "I'm such a loser!" Children with low self-esteem see themselves as somehow inadequate or even unlovable, which can be excruciatingly painful.

The Rise and Fall of the Self-Esteem Movement

In 1986, the governor of California created a Task Force on Self-Esteem and Personal and Social Responsibility with the hope that raising self-esteem would serve as a kind of mental vaccine, preventing problems such as crime, teen pregnancy, and drug abuse (Baumeister et al. 2003). Around the same time, leaders in education promoted the idea that boosting children's self-esteem would lead to higher achievement and better test scores. Numerous programs were created to try to foster high self-esteem in children (Harter 2017).

Unfortunately, but perhaps not surprisingly, trying to raise self-esteem didn't turn out to be a magical cure-all. Even research from the California task force showed very small relationships between self-esteem and the outcomes they hoped to produce. On the education front, some researchers began suggesting that promoting self-esteem could backfire by undermining children's motivation to learn or to try hard. (Why would kids try to improve if they're already wonderful?) Others argued that the focus on building up children's self-esteem takes away valuable time that educators could be using to teach skills. Also, children tend not to believe effusive praise (Damon 1995).

More recently, Jean Twenge and her colleagues (2008) have argued that an emphasis on cultivating high self-esteem has contributed to a generation of teens and young adults (born after 1980) being less empathic and more self-absorbed as well as more anxious and depressed than previous generations. However, other researchers have challenged these conclusions, arguing that the observed differences in self-centeredness reflect mainly a temporary developmental stage of life or methodological issues related to questionnaires and sample selection (Arnett, Trzesniewski, and Donnellan 2013).

We Don't Have to Love Ourselves

Still today, self-help gurus and inspirational articles often promote the idea that we have to love ourselves to have a happy, fulfilling life. This is nonsense. How many people honestly stand in front of a mirror and think, *I love myself!?* And if they do, would you want to be friends with those people? Probably not.

Logically, it makes sense that kids who feel better about themselves ought to do better in life, but that's not what research finds. Roy Baumeister and his colleagues (2003) conducted a very thorough research review and concluded that higher self-esteem does not cause better school performance. It does not prevent kids from smoking, drinking, using drugs, or engaging in early sexual activity. High self-esteem also does not lead to healthier relationships. In fact, bullies tend to have high self-esteem!

One reason that high self-esteem isn't necessarily linked to better outcomes is that it sometimes slips into narcissism. Narcissistic people don't just feel good about themselves; they think they are better than everyone else. They are convinced that they are special and therefore deserve special treatment. They are very self-centered, so they ignore, dismiss, or stomp on other people's feelings or wishes. If they do something kind, it's because they want to look good. They often brag and seek admiration, and they generally act as if they were performing in front of an audience.

Although narcissists report high self-esteem, their self-esteem is fragile. If they fail, if someone else performs better, if anyone criticizes them, or even if people don't admire them enthusiastically enough, they lash out in anger. They are quick to defend themselves and scornfully blame others when things go wrong.

This is certainly not how we want our children to be! Narcissists care more about looking good than being good. Their outward confidence has no depth.

Protecting Kids' Self-Esteem Can Backfire

Even kids who aren't overtly narcissistic can get caught in the trap of trying to "look good." When kids focus on protecting or increasing their self-esteem, it can backfire and set them up for failure. Imagine a student who's afraid that she will do badly on a test. Healthy coping strategies would be to start studying early and to ask for extra help from the teacher. But if the student is focused on protecting her self-esteem, she won't do that, because she won't want to look or feel "dumb." Instead, she'll put off studying until the last minute. That way, if she performs poorly on the test, she can protect her self-esteem by telling herself, *I didn't have enough time to study! I could have done better if I'd tried!* She'll also probably complain loudly about the unfairness of the test, the uselessness of the class, or the unhelpfulness of the teacher—anything to avoid facing the fact that she didn't know the material and didn't take steps to learn it.

Jennifer Crocker and her colleagues (2010) have investigated the high costs of pursuing self-esteem. They find that when a task seems very important to people's view of themselves, but they're not sure they can succeed, sometimes they deliberately won't try hard. Psychologists call this *self-handicapping*, which means setting up circumstances that guarantee failure but also provide an excuse for failure. Other possible self-defeating strategies to guard self-esteem include cheating, lying, hiding mistakes, making excuses, avoiding challenges, blaming or looking down on others, and responding angrily to criticism. Trying to look good can sometimes bring out the worst in people!

Why Self-Esteem Matters

So, if pursuing and protecting self-esteem tends to backfire, does this mean we should abandon the whole idea of self-esteem? No. We know from long-term studies that low self-esteem can be a risk factor for depression and eating disorders. Research by Ulrich Orth and his colleagues (2014) shows that low self-esteem isn't just a symptom of depression; it predicts and precedes depression at all ages, from childhood onwards.

Low self-esteem can also be emotionally painful. When kids hate themselves, their misery can feel intense, pervasive, and inescapable.

Low self-esteem can also lead to self-fulfilling prophecies. For example, a child who thinks other kids don't like him will avoid interactions with peers, which will make him seem unfriendly and lead to the rejection he fears.

Self-Esteem Boosting Strategies Don't Work

Many of the obvious strategies for trying to help kids with low self-esteem just plain don't work. For instance, telling kids they are wonderful can actually make kids with low self-esteem feel worse. In one study, Eddie Brummelman and his colleagues (2014b) had kids play a computer game. First, they did a noncompetitive practice round after which some kids got a text message telling them, "Wow, you're great!" Next, the kids played the game. Among kids who lost the game, those who had been told "You're great" before the defeat felt more ashamed than kids who hadn't been given this praise. This effect was especially pronounced for kids with low self-esteem. Hearing they were "great" set up kids with low self-esteem to feel "worthless, inferior, and exposed" when their actions didn't live up to the praise.

What about having kids tell themselves positive statements? Saying very positive things to themselves can make kids with low self-esteem feel bad about themselves, because they become acutely aware of how much they *don't* measure up to the positive statement. A study by Joanne Wood and her colleagues (2009) involving college students showed that prompting students with low self-esteem to repeat to themselves the statement "I'm a lovable person," or to focus on how that statement was true, made their moods worse rather than better, and made them feel *less* happy with themselves! Rather than boosting their self-esteem, this positive self-statement ended up highlighting and confirming their belief that they are not lovable.

Maybe kids with low self-esteem need to experience success to feel better about themselves. Nope. Kids with low self-esteem are experts at dismissing and discounting their victories. They pick apart their performance, insisting, "It wasn't *that* good. Anybody could have done it. And besides, I messed up one section." Another study by Joanne Wood and her colleagues (2005) found that people with low self-esteem feel more anxious after a victory than a defeat. They expected the defeat, but the victory seems surprising and dangerous.

Success usually doesn't penetrate low self-esteem, because it's hard to absorb and feels threatening for people who are used to viewing themselves as inadequate. Performing well tends to make kids with low self-esteem worry that they won't be able to keep up this performance, or that people will now expect more of them, or that people are now paying more attention to them, so their inevitable future failures will lead to increased public humiliation. Wood calls this "snatching defeat from the jaws of victory."

The reason all of these strategies for boosting self-esteem don't work is that they involve *increased self-focus*. They encourage kids with low self-esteem to think about and evaluate themselves, which they always do harshly, intensifying their misery.

What Real Self-Esteem Looks Like

The key to breaking free from low self-esteem is to move beyond self-focus. Real self-esteem isn't about believing we are special or wonderful. Real self-esteem means being able to let go of the question *Am I good enough?*

Think about how you feel when you get together with a close friend. Your friend knows you, warts and all, but you're not sitting there wondering, *Does my friend like me?* or *Is my friend impressed by me?* or *Is my friend going to dump me?* Those questions don't even come up, because you're not thinking about yourself. Instead, you're completely focused on the conversation or activity with this friend, which brings a satisfying sense of ease and comfort.

Real self-esteem involves developing this type of fully engaged presence in what we are doing right now. When we're not mentally standing back and judging ourselves, we are free to listen, and learn, and try, and experience, and do, and care...

So, how do we help kids with low self-esteem step beyond self-focus, so they can let go of their harsh self-evaluations? Research by Richard Ryan and his colleagues (2000, 2003) shows that the key is to address children's fundamental needs for what we'll call *connection*, *competence*, and *choice*. When these needs are met, children are less preoccupied with evaluating themselves and questioning their worth. Here's a look at each of these needs.

Connection

Connection involves building meaningful relationships that create a sense of belonging. Satisfying relationships with family and friends are an important part of real self-esteem because they pull children beyond self-focus toward caring for others. Also, when children feel known, accepted, and valued by others, it's easier for them not to question their worth. Love and concern for others—and just spending enjoyable time together—also give kids more interesting things to think about than their flaws.

Competence

Competence refers to gaining skills as well as learning how to learn, so children can do things that matter to them. For example, to have real self-esteem related to math, kids actually need to be able to *do* math problems and to know how to move forward when they hit a rough spot. They also need to understand that whatever skill level they have now is just a temporary stepping stone, because they have the capacity to grow and learn. Telling children that they're good at math, without helping them develop genuine competence, promotes wishful thinking that won't stand up to reality. On the other hand, when children are focused on learning and gaining competence, they're less likely to believe that their whole worth as a human being is on the line with every performance or to see mistakes as proof that they're inadequate.

Choice

Choice is about being able to make decisions, figure out what matters, and choose to act in ways that are consistent with personal values. No one likes to feel powerless or controlled by outside forces. Although children have far less opportunity than adults to decide what they want to do, they can still feel empowered by making choices. Choice allows children to muster internal motivation to move toward what is important to them, rather than stay mired in helplessness.

Wrap-Up and How to Use This Book

This book will *not* help you boost your child's self-esteem. Trying to convince kids that they're great is an ineffective, band-aid approach that doesn't penetrate the agonizing self-doubt and self-criticism experienced by children with low self-esteem.

Instead, this book offers a more powerful and nuanced approach that lets you guide your child away from the unhealthy self-focus that's the root cause of low self-esteem. The chapters about connection will show you how to help your child build strong and satisfying relationships with parents, siblings, and friends. The chapters about competence will look at ways to encourage your child to sustain effort, learn effectively, and let go of unhealthy perfectionism. The chapters on choice are about helping your child learn to make decisions and figure out personal values. When children are able to fulfill their fundamental needs for connection, competence, and choice, they're less apt to fret about their worth. They're too immersed in living their lives to dwell on judging themselves. That's real self-esteem.

This book will focus on ages six to twelve because these are the foundational years for building real self-esteem. Kids in this age range are old enough to think logically, but they tend to be more open than teens are to parental input. Self-esteem is also less stable in children than it is in teens and adults (Trzesniewski, Donnellan, and Robins 2003). Because children's self-views aren't written in stone, we have the opportunity to intervene to help ease harsh self-criticism.

There are many, many strategies in this book. Choose the ones that are a good fit for your child and your family. If you find that your child is continuing to feel unhappy and have low self-esteem for weeks or months, and especially if this is getting in the way of doing regular activities or leading to suicidal thoughts, please consult a mental health professional.

The next chapter will introduce developmental stages of self-esteem. I'll describe the earliest signs of thoughts about the self as well as how self-esteem changes as children grow older. It's handy to know what's typical for your child's age as well as what's ahead.

After that, I'll talk about common challenges that children with low self-esteem experience and specific ways that you, as a parent, can help. The title of each chapter in the main part of the book contains a statement that you may have heard your child say, representing a particular type of struggle related to low self-esteem. You can read the chapters in order or skip to the ones that seem most relevant for your child. There are also materials available for download at the website for this book: http://www.newharbinger.com/40491. (See the very back of this book for more details.)

There are many ways that children with low self-esteem get stuck because of their focus on judging themselves harshly and dwelling helplessly on their flaws. This book will show you ways to quiet that self-focus and ease your child toward more active, engaged, and satisfying ways of being in the world.

Take-Home Points

- Telling children with low self-esteem that they're wonderful can make them feel worse about themselves because it heightens their self-focus.

- Successes can be threatening—rather than confidence-building—for kids with low self-esteem.

- Helping children meet their fundamental needs for connection, competence, and choice is crucial to developing real self-esteem.

- Real self-esteem happens when children are able to let go of the question *Am I good enough?*

How Children's Self-Esteem Changes with Age

When does self-esteem begin? Clever experiments involving secretly putting a dot of rouge on a toddler's nose and then placing the toddler in front of a mirror, give us some clues about the beginnings of selfhood. Very young toddlers will reach for the mirror when they see the dot, but around eighteen months of age, toddlers recognize themselves in the mirror and will rub their own nose when they see the dot in the mirror (Rochat 2003). This means they have some sense of themselves as a person. They also have an idea of what is typical for them, or not, at least in terms of appearance. Between the ages of eighteen and twenty-seven months, children also start saying "I," "me," "my" and that delicious word "mine!" But toddlers certainly don't sit around judging themselves.

Susan Harter has interviewed hundreds of children to uncover how kids of different ages think about and judge themselves (Harter 2012). Drawing on her research, below I've named and described the main developmental stages, so you can see what's typical for kids of different ages. Understanding these stages will give you an overview of the normal ups and downs in self-esteem that children usually experience. Sometimes low self-esteem is part of a pattern for an individual child; sometimes it's just part of growing up. Knowing what's typical can give you a context for understanding what your child is going through.

The ages associated with each stage are approximate. You may find that your child is a little ahead or a little behind developmental trends.

Winding through each of the stages of self-esteem, you'll see connection, competence, and choice as recurring themes. At all ages, children care deeply about relationships and want to feel competent. They also show an increasing interest in making their own decisions about what matters to them and what they want to do. I'll highlight some red flags and mention some ideas about how parents can support children's real self-esteem at each stage, but we'll talk about these in more detail in later chapters.

Look-at-Me! Stage (Two to Four Years)

Some very self-conscious young children hate having attention focused on them, but most preschoolers are endearing little show-offs. They're in what I call the *Look-at-me! stage*. They have high self-esteem because they can't evaluate themselves objectively. They make grand claims like "I'm so fast!" or "I know all my ABCs" even when that's not true. They love an audience for their exploits, so they say things like, "Watch me do my big jumps!" as they bounce around the room.

Kids this age are very attuned to adult's reactions. They beam with pleasure and puff out their chests when adults praise them. On the flip side, they cringe in shame when they're scolded or when they can't master a task.

At this stage, children don't talk about having feelings about themselves, but their self-esteem can show in how they act. They might be reluctant to explore, or they might avoid challenges. They might cry and give up easily when they struggle. They might seem indifferent rather than proud of their work. All kids do these things sometimes. They're only a concern if they're part of a frequent, ongoing pattern.

General Tips

During the Look-at-me! stage, we can support our children's self-esteem by encouraging their curiosity and willingness to try new things and by expressing delight at their accomplishments. We don't have to agree with their evaluations that they are the biggest/fastest/ bestest, but we can freely comment on their effort, strategy, enjoyment, and progress. We can say things like "You kept working until you colored the whole thing!" "You really love jumping!" "Wow! You're getting better and better at cutting things out!"

We also need to be very gentle with young children when they misbehave. Toddlers do naughty things all day, every day. Redirecting them toward what they *should* do is kinder and more effective, in teaching children the right thing to do, than criticizing or punishing them. Although these little ones can't articulate any thoughts about self-esteem, they are beginning to gain a sense of themselves as capable or incapable, lovable or unlovable, based on their interactions with adults.

On-My-Way Stage (Five to Seven Years)

Next comes what I call the *on-my-way stage.* In the early elementary school years, children usually have high self-esteem because they like to compare what they can do *now* to what they did a year or two ago, and their progress is dramatic! This is a stage of rapidly expanding skills. Compared to a four-year-old, a six-year-old can ride a bike, read and write words, do simple math, play board games, and throw a ball with far greater accuracy. These big changes are thrilling for kids!

Kids this age care a lot about fairness. They compare themselves to others mostly to see if they are being treated fairly, rather than to evaluate themselves.

Children in the on-my-way stage understand that other people judge them, and they begin to form ideas of themselves as good or bad at certain activities. For the most part, they're still unrealistically positive about their abilities. Although kids this age don't talk about overall self-esteem, recent research shows that even children as young as five years old have a general sense of their personal qualities. When asked to sort words according to whether they are "me" or "not me," five-year-olds can describe themselves as fun, good, happy, and nice, rather than bad, mad, mean, or yucky (Cvencek, Greenwald, and Meltzoff 2016). Also, their self-esteem can drop if they see that they are noticeably behind other kids in developing certain skills, such as reading or swimming.

As they're trying to navigate their expanding world, kids this age tend to be rigid thinkers. They say things like "That's babyish!" or "That's for girls!" Seeing the world in simple either-or categories makes it easier to understand, but it also leads to strong opinions about what they do or don't want to do and what other kids should or shouldn't do. Kids whose interests don't fit stereotypes may struggle to fit in.

Friendship is a big part of self-esteem at this age. In these early elementary years, children care deeply about having friends, but they're not so good at being friends, because they have trouble imagining how other people feel. They play well one minute and argue the next. They may have a best friend, but their friendships often shift. They're frequently bossy and critical, but their feelings are easily hurt when a peer criticizes or excludes them. It's common for kids this age to cheat or to quit in a huff when a game isn't going their way. They're also likely to lie to avoid getting in trouble (but it's usually obvious when they do so).

Unlike younger kids, elementary school children have developed a sense of self with a life story of past events that are connected to their current situation and have implications for their future. Young elementary school children also enjoy imagining grand future plans, such as becoming an astronaut, a veterinarian, or a famous rock star...maybe all at the same time, and preferably doing all of these jobs with their friends!

Warning signs of possible problems with low self-esteem at this age might include not being able to describe something they can do well or not expressing dreams for the future. Kids who often call themselves "stupid," "mean," or "bad" and who seem sad, irritable, or unenergetic need help to address their low self-esteem.

General Tips

During the on-my-way stage, the best thing we can do as parents to support our children's self-esteem is to help them master new skills and to be enthusiastic about their progress. Children this age want very much to please their parents. We also need to give them lots of opportunities to be with friends. One-on-one playdates outside of school are important for developing friendships. When conflict flares, we can help our kids work out a compromise or provide a distraction by asking a timely question such as "Who wants a snack?" to get them past the rough patch.

Judging-Myself Stage (Eight to Ten Years)

For many children, issues with self-esteem flare up around age eight to ten, during the *judging-myself stage*. At this age, children have developed enough thinking skills to be able to realistically compare themselves to others, so they see that they're *not* always the best at what they do. This means they generally see themselves in a more negative light than younger children do, and they may develop feelings of inadequacy.

Kids this age are often harshly self-critical. They're very aware of the gap between how they want to be and how they actually are. It's hard for them to understand that learning is a process and building skills takes time. If they're not immediately successful at some activity, they jump to the conclusion that they're "no good" at doing it.

To protect their self-esteem, kids in the judging-myself stage can also be defensive. They say things like "I'm bad at sports, but I don't care! Sports are stupid!" Trying hard at something they're struggling to learn can make them feel uncomfortably exposed.

In the judging-myself stage, children recognize that they can have both positive and negative qualities at the same time, but it could be a red flag if they see mainly their weaknesses balanced by few strengths. They may resort to a variety of unhealthy strategies to enhance their self-esteem. For instance, some children try to make themselves feel good by putting others down. Some hang out mainly with kids they can dominate or impress. Still others become enraged when they are criticized. Routinely using one or more of these unhealthy strategies could be a sign of low or fragile self-esteem.

General Tips

As parents, the best way we can support self-esteem during this stage is to try to soften their harsh judgments. When our child says, "I can't do anything right!" we can say "You're struggling with *this* activity right *now*." We can offer support to help them keep trying or express our confidence that they'll be able to figure things out if they stick with it. We can also help them recognize their progress. When they make a mistake, we should give them a chance to make it right. They need to be able to have a path forward instead of feeling stuck being "bad." Children this age usually look up to their parents, so sharing stories of our past struggles can be inspiring and reassuring to them.

Trying-to-Look-Good Stage (Eleven to Thirteen Years)

The middle school years, ages eleven to thirteen, are what I call the *trying-to-look-good stage*. During this stage, kids are often excruciatingly self-conscious, and their self-esteem tends to be lower than in earlier stages. They worry a lot about what other people think of them and where they fit in the social pecking order. Younger kids might say, "I'm bad at math!" but middle schoolers tend to say, "My math teacher hates me!" when the math teacher really only reminded them to be sure to show their work.

Bodily changes related to puberty—or a lack of those changes—adds to self-consciousness during the trying-to-look-good stage. Kids this age are very concerned with being "normal," and they report that their self-esteem is based mainly on how they feel about their appearance. They tend to spend a lot of time in front of the mirror critically examining every inch of their appearance. And it's not just girls who have a long list of their supposed physical flaws. Increasingly, boys are preoccupied with physical appearance—such as wanting to have "six-pack abs"—and painfully aware of how they fall short of what they believe counts as the physical ideal.

This stage marks the beginning of what psychologists call the *imaginary audience* (Elkind 1967). Because kids this age are preoccupied with evaluating every little bit of how they look and what they do, they assume that other people are as well. They believe that everyone is constantly looking at them closely and judging everything about them, which makes them feel like they are performing on stage. They may try to fit in by dressing and acting exactly the same as everyone else in their peer group. They may also spend a lot of time ruminating about possible social mistakes.

To adults, all this focus on what others think may seem silly or overblown, but research tells us that, for young adolescents, the opinions of peers have real personal and social consequences. Other kids really are judging them constantly, and not necessarily kindly (Bell and Bromnick 2003). Although some studies suggest that concern about the imaginary audience peaks in eighth grade (Alberts, Elkind, and Ginsberg 2007), others find that, on average, this concern stays high until after age thirty (Frankenberger 2000). This means it doesn't make sense to tell young adolescents, "Don't worry about what other people think!" That's just not possible for them. However, they might be able to consider the source. Ask your child, "Are these people whose opinion matters to you? Do you trust their judgment? Do they play an important role in your life?" Questions such as these could help your child inch toward understanding that different people might have different perspectives, and not all opinions are equally valid or meaningful.

At this stage, because children's self-esteem is so dependent on interpreting, remembering, guessing, or anticipating the reactions of others, it can swing up and down wildly. One minute they feel smart and cool; the next minute they feel stupid and awkward. Support from close friends and family can help lessen these swings.

Texting, online gaming, and social media activities often begin in the middle-school years and intensify in high school. New dangers such as privacy threats and cyberbullying emerge, but for most kids, online activities support and extend their face-to-face friendships. It can be very comforting for kids to know their friends are as close as their back pockets.

One recent study that looked at the social media activity of thirteen-year-olds found that 84 percent of these kids say that social media makes them feel good about themselves at least sometimes, and only 19 percent say social media makes them feel bad about themselves at least sometimes (Underwood and Faris 2015). Social media gives kids a venue to present a positive image of themselves to the world. On the other hand, it also means that self-conscious tweens and teens are subject to a whole different level of public exposure as well as unlimited opportunity to compare themselves to others. This can sometimes lead to a sense that "everyone else" has a much more exciting and interesting life. We also know that frequent checking of social media is linked to distress. However, it's not clear whether unhappy kids check social media more often or their checking social media more often leads to their being unhappy, or some other factor such as shyness or loneliness leads to both more distress and more social-media checking.

Red flags in the trying-to-look-good stage could include a lack of supportive friends or painful self-consciousness that makes kids avoid being around peers. Another concern is when online activity eclipses face-to-face interaction with peers. With their growing focus on independence, relationships with peers are even more important for kids at this age than they were for younger kids. But relationships with parents don't lessen in importance. We still matter to our children—a lot.

General Tips

You can play a very important role in supporting real self-esteem at this stage by helping your child find enjoyable activities and groups to join. You can also be an important counterweight to some of the shallow values and unrealistic standards that pervade popular culture. Remind your child that it doesn't make sense to compare how she feels on the inside to what someone else looks like on the outside. Although your child might dismiss your remarks, she'll also take comfort in your steady presence and the fact that you see her through loving eyes.

Trying-to-Be-Myself Stage (Fourteen to Sixteen Years)

Ages fourteen to sixteen correspond to the *trying-to-be-myself stage*, which tends to be an especially difficult period for kids in terms of self-esteem. Teens this age spend a lot of time trying to figure out who they "really" are. They don't want to be phony, so they're deeply bothered by the fact that they act differently with different people or in different situations. They agonize over trying to decide if they're really kind or mean, outgoing or shy, hardworking or lazy. They view themselves as complicated and unique. They're often convinced that no one can understand them—especially not their parents.

This is the age where we start to see dramatic differences in rates of depression between boys and girls. Starting around age thirteen, rates of depression in girls—but not boys—increase markedly. By late adolescence, girls are twice as likely as boys to be depressed

(Nolen-Hoeksema 2001). Although it's not uncommon for teens this age to be moody or withdrawn around parents, being that way around peers as well could be cause for concern. Red flags for depression in teens include feeling sad or irritable most of the time, feeling worthless, having excessive or inappropriate guilt, being tired all the time or having noticeably less energy, losing interest in activities they used to enjoy, having difficulty concentrating, and/or experiencing changes in sleep, weight, or appetite. Some teens also become involved in drinking, drugs, or sexual activity in an attempt to fit in or to manage their unhappiness.

General Tips

Give your child room to try on different identities, but also insist on reasonable limits to keep your child safe. If you need to correct your child, do it gently and offer a way to make amends. Avoid bringing up anything your child did more than a month ago, because kids this age are working hard to construct a new sense of self, and they don't want to be burdened by their past mistakes or childish words or actions. Also avoid making negative predictions about your child's future. Saying or implying to teens, "Get it together, or you'll never amount to anything!" is cruel and definitely not helpful. Show unwavering faith that your child will find a path that's right for him or her. Be there as a secure base from which your child can launch and as a source of comfort during the inevitable rough patches.

Self-Esteem in Young Adulthood and Beyond

Around age seventeen is a turning point for kids' self-esteem. The self-contradictions that were so worrisome for younger teens feel more manageable for older teens because they see themselves in a more complex, multifaceted way. They understand and accept that it's possible to be, for example, both outgoing and shy, depending on the situation. Their self-esteem is also less dependent on how people view them because they have a clearer sense of who they are and what matters to them.

Beyond the teen years, average self-esteem levels increase noticeably in the mid- to late twenties and again in our fifties and sixties, before dropping after age seventy (Robins et al. 2002). Unfortunately, it's not particularly comforting to tell a child or teen who is struggling with low self-esteem, "Don't worry! In about five decades, you'll probably feel pretty good about yourself!"

General Trends and Your Particular Child

On top of the general developmental trends, there are individual differences between children of the same age. Long-term studies tell us that children who have lower self-esteem compared to their peers at one age also tend to have lower self-esteem at later ages (Tevendale and DuBois 2006). Once children have formed a mental picture of how others view them, that picture influences how they behave and how they interpret other people's responses. They tend to think and act in ways that confirm their original view of themselves (Wallace and Tice 2012). If they expect to be rejected, they'll be on the lookout for signs of rejection and won't bother to act friendly. If they expect to fail, they'll avoid trying. Their self-criticism can become a self-fulfilling prophecy.

Wrap-Up

On average, children's self-esteem tends to be unrealistically high at very young ages then go downhill through the school years, with noticeable drops around ages eight and in the early and middle adolescent years. I don't think it's a coincidence that this drop in children's self-esteem is paralleled by increasing self-focus. As kids get older, their views of themselves become more complicated, they spend more time thinking about and evaluating themselves, and they tend to become more self-critical. (In contrast, adults' expanding roles and responsibilities tend to draw their attention outward, toward family, colleagues, clients, community, social causes, and other concerns.)

So, does the general downward trend in self-esteem for children mean you should try to increase your child's self-esteem? No. Trying to get kids to feel good about themselves is a trap. It keeps them stuck, constantly judging and comparing themselves to others. In the coming chapters, we'll talk about ways you can lessen your child's self-focus by emphasizing connection, competence, and choice.

The next three chapters in this book look at important relationships in your child's life. The intimacy and support that kids get from their parents, siblings, and friends contribute to them feeling known and valued and to being less preoccupied with judging themselves. These relationships are an important foundation for real self-esteem.

Take-Home Points

- Understanding the ages and stages of development gives you a better idea of normal ups and downs of children's self-esteem.

- Self-esteem is rocky from preschool through age sixteen, and then it improves.

- Specific development stages that involve increased self-focus (like adolescence) tend to result in dips in self-esteem.

PART 2
CONNECTION

"Why Are You Always Yelling at Me?"

When Your Child Reacts Intensely to Parental Correction

"I can't believe you did that!" David's mother said as they got into the car. She slammed the car door closed. "How many times have I told you before? When I say it's time to leave a friend's house, you need to just leave, without making a big fuss!"

"Well, you and Marco's mom kept talking," David objected. "And it wasn't just me fooling around. Marco started it! He pretended to wipe a booger on me, so I pretended to wipe it back on him…We were just having fun!"

"But Marco wasn't the one who knocked a picture on the floor and broke the glass!"

"I said I was sorry," David insisted.

"You muttered a one-word apology, without even looking at his mom. I was the one who apologized again and again and offered to clean up. And that doesn't fix the picture, does it? Do you think she is going to want to have you over again when you act wild and break her stuff?"

"I dunno," David mumbled.

"No video games for the rest of the week for you!"

David began to cry. "Why are you always yelling at me? You think I'm the worst kid in the world!" he said.

"I'm not yelling. I'm just disappointed in your behavior," David's mom insisted.

●

This is a difficult situation for David and his mother. Clearly, David did a bad thing by breaking the picture. But let's consider the emotions that are probably underlying this interaction: both David and his mom are feeling ashamed.

David responds initially by trying to deflect blame: the moms were chatting; Marco was the one who started it. Then he shifts toward defensiveness ("I said I was sorry!"), then dejection, and finally anger and hurt as he accuses his mother of not liking him.

David's mom probably felt mortified that her child behaved so badly in front of another adult. Parents tend to feel responsible when their kids do something wrong. Maybe she imagined Marco's mother judging her, thinking *What kind of a mom are you to allow your kid to behave so badly?* But for David's mom, the shame comes out as anger toward David.

Parents walk a fine line. On the one hand, we want our kids to feel unconditionally loved and accepted. On the other hand, it's our job to teach them to pick up their socks, finish their homework, use a napkin rather than their shirtsleeve, and stop poking their sister. It's unrealistic to imagine that we'll always be pleased with our children. Plus, our feedback, both positive and negative, is vitally important for children to learn our values and understand what is or isn't acceptable behavior.

Finding the balance between connection and correction isn't always easy. Emotions were flying high in the heated exchange between Marco and his mom, but for children with low self-esteem, sometimes even very mild corrections from a parent can send them into a spiral of self-criticism and claims of being unloved.

This chapter will look at how our reactions to our children's behavior influence how they feel about themselves. It will also explore how we can harness the strength of our connection with our children to ease them away from harsh self-criticism.

Why Some Kids Are More Prone to Low Self-Esteem

When children struggle with low self-esteem, parents often feel anxious and guilty. They wonder, *Did I cause this? Have I been too critical? Am I not supportive enough? Is it because I lost my temper that time?* The good news and the bad news is it's usually not that simple.

Low self-esteem arises from a combination of inborn temperamental tendencies and negative life experiences. We know that there's a genetic contribution to self-esteem (Hart, Atkins, and Tursi 2006). But there's no gene that causes people to hate themselves. We know that children who have been abused are more likely to experience shame and low self-esteem (Harter 2015). However, the vast majority of parents of children with low self-esteem are definitely not abusive.

Temperament and experience combine to create many paths to low self-esteem. For instance, a child like David who was born with a tendency to be active and impulsive probably gets in trouble with adults and irritates peers more than other kids. Consistently receiving negative social feedback is likely to affect how he feels about himself. Or imagine a child who is anxious and extremely sensitive to criticism. This child might be prone to remembering and ruminating about the slightest scolding, leading to low self-esteem. Still another child might be a poor student or a poor athlete compared to classmates, which triggers a sense of inadequacy that solidifies into low self-esteem.

Seeing Themselves Through Others' Eyes

An important early theory of self-esteem is Cooley's idea of "the looking glass self" ([1902] 1983). This theory claims that we develop a sense of ourselves through our interactions with others. We imagine how others perceive us, judge us, and feel about us, which evokes thoughts and feelings about ourselves.

As parents, we are our children's first mirrors and an enduring influence on how they see themselves. When we react to our children with delight or amusement or disapproval or compassion, their perceptions of our reactions contribute to their growing understanding of who they are, which affects how they feel about themselves. Although the importance of teacher and peer approval increases as kids get older, the impact of parent approval on self-esteem doesn't drop from early childhood through adolescence (Harter 1990).

Development of Self-Conscious Emotions

As children develop, they learn to internalize the standards of important others. This evokes *self-conscious emotions* in them, which are feelings about the self that stem from judgments of the self. Self-conscious emotions include shame, guilt, and pride. These emotions are the heat behind self-esteem, so let's look at how they develop.

Toddlers sometimes seem upset when their parents are displeased with them. They look down or look away, and they may even cry when they know they're in trouble. Preschoolers can predict what will make their parents happy or mad, but it takes many years and a lot of cognitive development before kids can muster the complicated judgments behind fully formed self-conscious emotions.

In one study, Susan Harter (2015) showed children a story with pictures involving a child character stealing some coins from a large jar in the parents' bedroom. In one version of the story, no one finds out about the theft. In the other version, the parent sees the child take the coins. Harter asked children of different ages how they and their parents would feel in each situation. Four-year-olds responded to the story by saying that they would feel worried about getting caught if the parents didn't see them steal or they'd be afraid of being punished if the parents did see them steal. They made no mention of shame. Five-year-olds said their parents would feel ashamed of them if they saw the theft, but they didn't talk about feeling ashamed of themselves. Six-year-olds said they would feel ashamed of themselves, but only if their parents saw the theft. As one boy explained, "If I did something bad, I *might* be able to feel ashamed if I was all by myself, but it would sure help if my parents found out!" (p. 208) Seven-year-olds talked about feeling ashamed of themselves if they stole the money, even if their parents didn't catch them.

Harter found similar results for stories involving feeling proud of doing a new gymnastics feat. As kids grew older, they shifted from being simply happy, to being aware of their parents' pride, to feeling proud of themselves when their parents watched, to finally feeling proud of their accomplishment even without an audience.

So, young children notice and remember how people, especially parents, react to them. Over time, their perception of these reactions contribute to forming the standards by which children come to judge themselves as well as their feelings about themselves. Unfortunately, just saying good things about our kids doesn't guarantee that they'll feel good about themselves.

Distorting Social Mirrors

When we look in an ordinary physical mirror, we see a direct and accurate reflection of ourselves, but social mirrors are more complicated. Kids don't just passively absorb what others express about them. They weigh certain people's opinions more heavily than others. Also, their interpretations of others' reactions are colored by what they already believe about themselves (Swann and Seyle 2006).

Children with low self-esteem tend to see social feedback through a negative filter. They're quick to dismiss praise, and they're on the lookout for signs of criticism and rejection because that's what they expect to receive.

For instance, you may have tried to reassure your daughter that she's smart or talented or athletic and had her dismiss your comments by remarking, "You have to say that because you're my parent!"

On the flip side, children with low self-esteem are prone to hearing ordinary or minor criticism, turning it into condemnation of their entire worth as a human being, and plummeting into painful shame. That's where David went when he told his mom, "You think I'm the worst kid in the world!"

Understanding the Difference Between Shame and Guilt

When children sense or imagine that they've done something to make others view them negatively, they often experience feelings of shame or guilt. Both of these emotions motivate children (and adults) to avoid and repent wrongdoing. They're like an inner alarm, giving immediate and very noticeable internal feedback when we fall short of social standards of what is good, right, or acceptable.

However, there are important differences between these emotions. Guilt comes from thinking *I did a bad thing.* Shame stems from an all-encompassing judgment that *I'm a bad person.* This seems like a subtle distinction, but research tells us that these two emotions involve very different experiences and behavior (Tangney and Tracy 2012).

Guilt is an uncomfortable pinch of conscience. It's linked to feeling remorse and being motivated to fix the situation somehow. Guilt makes people want to apologize or make amends. In general, guilt-prone people tend to be empathic, caring, and good at perspective taking. When they get angry, they usually manage to respond constructively rather than resorting to aggression.

Shame, on the other hand, is excruciatingly painful. When people are ashamed, they feel exposed, inadequate, and even worthless. They want to escape or hide. They wish the ground would open up beneath them, so they could just disappear. The agonizing self-focus of shame crushes self-esteem and also gets in the way of caring about others. In fact, people who are feeling ashamed tend to spew blame and lash out aggressively. Whereas guilt motivates relationship repair, shame-based reactions tend to damage or even destroy relationships. Shame-proneness is linked to a wide range of problems, including anxiety, depression, eating disorders, and low self-esteem (Mills 2005).

However, we can't just conclude that guilt is good and shame is bad. Although they can be separated conceptually and statistically, in real life, these two emotions often occur in a messy blend along the lines of *I did a bad thing, which means I'm a bad person.* Guilt can also be excessive or inappropriate. For instance, you may have heard your child insist, "I'm sorry! I'm sorry! I'm sorry!" for a minor mishap or something that wasn't even your child's fault.

There are also cultural differences related to self-conscious emotions. In one study, children in grades three through six, in three different countries, completed a scenario-based questionnaire about self-conscious emotions. Japanese children reported experiencing more shame, Korean children more guilt, and US children more pride (Furukawa, Tangney, and Higashibara 2012). However, in all three countries, shame-prone children were more likely to get angry and blame others, so there is also some cross-cultural consistency in the experience and impact of these emotions.

How Shame and Guilt Influence Children's Self-Esteem

All kids sometimes feel ashamed or guilty, but research consistently shows a link between the tendency to experience shame and low self-esteem. Guilt proneness, on the other hand, is *not* linked to low self-esteem (Tangney and Tracy 2012). When children feel healthy guilt, they can acknowledge and address misdeeds without beating themselves up or feeling worthless.

Why We Need to Manage Our Own Shame and Guilt

Before we talk about how to address children's shame and guilt, we need to address *parental* shame and guilt. While responding gently to our children's mistakes is crucial, it's equally important to be compassionate with ourselves, as parents. By forgiving ourselves, we can teach our kids to do the same.

I worked with a family once where the girl tended to react impulsively when she was frustrated. One day, she hit another kid at school. The incident was serious enough to warrant a trip to the principal's office. When she heard about this, the girl's mother was horrified. She wasn't even there when it happened, but she felt responsible. Although her daughter wrote a note of apology to the child she'd hit, this mother felt she needed to reach out to the other mom as well. She expected to be greeted with hostility and criticism, but she called anyway to see how the child was doing and to apologize for her daughter's behavior. The other mother assured her that the child was fine. Then she did something very kind. She said, "This parenting thing is hard." With that small statement of empathy and connection, she relieved the other mom of her shame and guilt over her daughter's behavior.

I mention this story because that's the kind of compassion we need to work toward for ourselves as well as our children. No parent is perfect. We've all had times when we've reacted to our kids with impatience, frustration, and anger. I'm definitely not suggesting that we shrug off or dismiss hurtful actions. What I am saying is that being harshly critical of ourselves or our kids isn't helpful.

When—not if—your child messes up, try to respond gently, in ways that help your child move forward. And when—not if—you do or say things with your child that you regret, focus on moving forward. You may be able to model a genuine apology for your child, or you may want to come up with a plan for how to handle that situation differently next time. Love means trying again.

Real Self-Esteem Tips to Try

So, how do we help kids with low self-esteem both learn our values and go easier on themselves? Hint number one is that you *don't* have to be a perfect parent with saint-like patience. However, it does help to have a game plan, so you can respond to your child's bad as well as good behavior in ways that support the development of real self-esteem. Here are some strategies.

Helpful Responses to Misbehavior

One of our most important jobs as parents is to teach our kids how to be in relationships. This requires that we offer them a combination of both warmth and limits. Kids need warmth from us because that's the foundation of relationships and of self-acceptance. They also need limits, so they can step beyond self-interest and toward caring about others. Children have to understand how what they do affects other people and, more pragmatically, to learn what kinds of behaviors other people will and won't tolerate. To be blunt, if your kid routinely acts like a jerk, other people are not going to respond well to this. Knowing that we, their parents, are their safety guardrails, preventing them from going too far in a not-good direction, gives kids a sense of security.

When we're feeling angry with our children, when we imagine that they are deliberately trying to disrespect us, or when we're ashamed of what their behavior might make others think of us, it's all too easy to lash out harshly. It's very human to want our kids to suffer when they've caused us to suffer! But that's not an effective way to help kids learn.

Here are two guiding principles that are my touchstones for figuring out how to discipline kids:

1. We can't help children move forward by convincing them of their badness.

2. Children learn, not through suffering, but by doing it right.

Let's take a look at what these principles mean, in practical terms, for responding to children's misbehavior.

Cool Down, Then Connect

In the opening story, probably the best thing that David's mom could have done was to say "I'm too upset to talk about this right now."

You don't have to respond in the heat of the moment. In fact, it's almost always best if you don't! If tempers are running high, give yourself—and your child—time and space to cool off.

How do you know when you've cooled down enough? It's when you're able to imagine the situation from your child's perspective.

No kid is bad to the bone. Maybe your child got carried away, reacted without thinking, or just didn't know a better way to solve a problem. Maybe your child was tired or hungry or in a difficult situation. None of this makes the misbehavior acceptable, but if you can see things from your child's perspective, you're in a better place to help your child move forward.

Once she was feeling calmer, David's mom could have focused first on connecting with him by acknowledging his view of things. She could have said something like "You're probably feeling pretty bad about how things ended at Marco's house" or "I know you didn't mean to break that picture."

By reaching out to our kids with kindness after they've messed up, we can ease their shame. A gentle and compassionate response from us doesn't mean we approve of what they did, but it opens the way for them to make better choices and to feel appropriate guilt rather than shame for their actions.

Offer Soft Criticism

Criticism is hard to take. It's hard for us adults, and it's even harder for kids. The instinctive response to criticism is to defend or deflect by blaming others. That's exactly what David did.

One common piece of advice is to criticize the behavior and not the child. If we think in terms of shame and guilt, it's certainly better to tell children "You did a bad thing" than to tell them "You're a bad kid." However, as someone who has spoken with many, many children in my psychotherapy practice, I can tell you that most children can't hear the difference between these two remarks. As adults, we're pretty good at rationalizing *Well, I did that one bad thing, but overall, I'm a pretty good person.* But kids are black-and-white thinkers. When they're confronted with having done something bad, they feel *totally* bad.

Another common piece of advice is to sandwich criticism between two positive remarks. That doesn't really work, either. Think of your last performance evaluation at work. Your boss might have said twelve positive things, but it's that one little criticism that you stew over. Negative information stands out far more than positive comments.

So, what can we do instead? How can we give our kids necessary corrective feedback in a way that they can hear it? We can use what I call *soft criticism*, which has three steps:

1. Give an excuse. Think of a legitimate reason why your child might have done whatever the misbehavior was. This gets around defensiveness. If you *give* your child an excuse, he doesn't have to come up with one. Examples of possible excuses include

"I know you didn't mean to…"

"You probably didn't realize…"

"I understand that you have a lot going on…"

"I get that you were trying to…"

The excuse says to your child, *I know you're a good person, with good intentions, even when you make mistakes.* Also, in order to come up with an excuse, you have to stop and consider the situation from your child's point of view, which will raise your empathy and lower your anger.

2. Describe the problem. This is the part that we're itching to get to, but we need to do it gently. Tell your child, "…but, when you [bad behavior], [bad outcome]." For the bad-behavior part, briefly say what your child did ("when you hit your brother…" or "took her sweater without asking…" or "left the milk out…"). Keep the criticism focused on specific, observable actions rather than personality. For the bad-outcome part, describe how your child's behavior affected someone else or brought about some problem. Paint a vivid picture here, so your child can imagine someone else's feelings. The bad outcome could be something along the lines of "He felt very hurt because …" or "I felt frustrated because…"

3. Move forward. Helping kids find a path forward after they've done something wrong is crucial. Kids can't undo what they've already done, but we don't want to leave them stuck feeling bad about themselves. Moving forward could involve apologizing, making amends, or making positive plans.

Lectures don't work, because kids tend to tune them out, but thoughtful questions can help your child come up with a plan for moving forward. For instance, you could ask, "What can you do to help him feel better?" This is such a wonderful question! It empowers kids to act in caring ways. It implies that—despite recent actions—they care about others, and they have the ability to do good in the world. Also, acts of kindness are more meaningful when kids choose them rather than have adults impose them.

Other useful questions for moving forward include "What can you do to solve this problem?" "What can we do to prevent this from happening?" "What might make it easier for you to handle that situation?" or "What could you do instead, the next time you're in that situation?"

If your child has trouble coming up with a way to move forward, you could ask more specific questions ("What could you do to let her know that you're sorry?") or present a couple of options ("Would you rather call or write a note?")

Sometimes, you just need to ask directly, "From now on, could you please...?" but when kids can come up with their own solution, they're more invested in having that solution work.

Putting the three steps of a soft criticism together, David's mom might have said:

Step 1. Give excuse: "I know you were just having fun with Marco, and you didn't mean to break anything."

Step 2. Describe problem: "But when you knocked the picture off the wall, Marco's mother looked very upset. I think that picture was important to her, because it was right there in the front hall."

Step 3. Move forward: "What could you do to help her feel better?"

Focus on Prevention

Focusing on prevention is kinder and more helpful than correcting kids after they've done something bad. We can never do this perfectly, but when we think ahead and work with our children to prepare them to cope with likely difficulties, we help them manage their world better and avoid shame. If your child is headed into a challenging situation, on the way there, ask, "What do you need to remember to do in this situation?" Let your child tell you the answer, so it's right at the front of your child's mind before entering the situation.

If there's a situation that's routinely difficult for your child, talk together at some neutral time to plan how to make things work better. State the problem in terms of multiple concerns ("On the one hand… On the other hand…"). Ask your child for ideas of how to solve the problem. If your child suggests something unreasonable (such as siblings should move out), don't let yourself get derailed. Just say neutrally, "Well, that's one possibility, but it doesn't solve the part about [the problem]. What else could we do?"

Avoid Harsh Consequences

But what about consequences for bad behavior? Most parents hearing the word "discipline" assume it means inflicting negative consequences on children. Actually, *discipline* means "teach."

Some kids are very easy to discipline. They follow instructions and respect rules. If they get off course, you pretty much just have to raise an eyebrow, and they fall in line. Other kids are more challenging. They're louder, more boisterous, more emotional, and they push the boundaries more. These children often need parents to step in to insist that they take a short break to cool down. Children can't learn or even think when they're flooded with emotion, and it's often easier for them to calm down—and avoid doing something they'll regret—if they can step out of a volatile situation for a while.

Being able to step away from a heated situation is a useful life skill. Plan with your child what he can do when he needs to take a break to calm down. Activities involving the senses are often helpful. These could include looking through a kaleidoscope, listening to a rain stick, smelling unlit scented candles, or stroking a soft blanket or stuffed animal. You may want to work with your child to set up a box of calming items, so they're ready when needed.

Allowing children to experience natural consequences that stem automatically from their behavior sometimes make sense. These could include being late because they dawdled or doing without some item for a while because they broke it or used it inappropriately. But here's a very important thing to remember: negative consequences don't help children learn the *right* way to behave. The learning starts when we tell our kids, "Okay, let's try again." Planning may be necessary to make sure that trying again goes better than it did before, but giving your kid another chance is an expression of faith in her ability to learn.

Avoid long or harsh punishments. They build resentment and delay learning. I strongly recommend against taking away birthdays, holidays, contact with friends, or the out-of-home activity that your child loves most. You don't want your child to spend a lifetime remembering, *That was the year I was so bad, my parents took away Halloween.* Harsh punishments are a reflection of our anger, and they're not useful for helping children do better next time. They also tend to trigger resentment and shame.

Instead, when your child makes a mistake, focus on finding a way for him to make amends. This might involve doing an act of kindness for a parent or sibling. Hard physical labor for kids can also be a good means of making amends. Surely you have recycling to sort, laundry to fold, a garden to weed, or some other project your child could do! You may want to offer a choice of two options for making amends. When your child exerts effort to make things better for others, and you come in afterward and say, "Wow! That looks great! Thank you," you've gotten your child back on the track of being a good kid.

Develop Amnesia for Past Sins

One of the most generous things we can do as parents is to develop amnesia for our children's prior misbehavior. Children are growing and changing so rapidly, whatever they did last month was pretty much done by an entirely different person. So it doesn't make sense to bring it up again.

Encouraging Responses to Positive Behavior

Up to this point, our focus has been on how to respond to children's misbehavior to minimize self-esteem-crushing shame. But how we respond when kids behave well is also important for their self-esteem.

Authentic pride is a self-conscious emotion related to the judgment *I did a good thing!* Initially, kids feel pride when they do something that gets a positive reaction from their parents or other important people in their lives. Eventually, they internalize standards and feel proud of accomplishments even when no one is around to praise them.

The flip side of shame versus guilt is arrogance versus authentic pride. Like shame, arrogance involves judgments about the whole self and a lack of concern for others; like guilt, authentic pride focuses on specific actions and motivates positive social responses. Feeling proud makes kids want to do more of what lead to approval from people who matter to them.

Children with low self-esteem struggle to embrace authentic pride. One mistake can eclipse everything else they've ever done. You may have heard your child dismiss accomplishments by listing all the ways whatever she did wasn't perfect. (Perfectionism is covered in chapter 7.)

Some children adopt arrogance as a defense against shame. They may brag frequently, which is off-putting to their peers. Their outward strutting is paper-thin. When they don't perform well or when someone outperforms them, their fragile self-esteem crumbles, and they lash out in shame-fueled anger.

Let's look at some ways to respond to our children when they behave well, so they can more easily experience authentic pride.

Be Pleasable

Among my saddest clients are those who say, "Nothing I do or did is ever good enough for my parents." I don't think we ever outgrow our wish for our parents to be proud of us.

Make sure that your child knows that it's possible to please you. Our kids' misbehavior tends to be obvious, but it takes deliberate effort on our part to catch our kids being good.

Unrealistic expectations can get in the way of being pleasable. It's all too easy to get tangled up thinking about what most children do or about what kids ought to be able to do, or even about what siblings/cousins/friends do. None of that is relevant. Each child is unique. Realistic expectations focus on what this particular child does *most of the time* at this particular point in development…or just a bit beyond what's typical for this child.

For instance, kids "should" do their homework every evening, capably and without fussing. Some children manage this easily. Some need extra support to get started or to keep going or to avoid distractions. Being pleasable means recognizing and acknowledging genuine effort and improvement for your particular child.

Avoid Inflated Praise

It seems logical that showering children with high praise ought to help them feel good about themselves, but this tactic tends to backfire when kids have low self-esteem. Research by Eddie Brummelman and his colleagues (2016) tells us that parents are about twice as likely to give children with low self-esteem (rather than high self-esteem) inflated praise. They say, for example, "You did an amazing job!" rather than "You did a good job!" However, this type of praise tends to make children with low self-esteem feel uncomfortably self-conscious and worried about not being able to maintain such exceptional performance.

For example, in one study, Brummelman and his colleagues (2014a) invited children to draw a picture. They then told the children either "You made an *incredibly* beautiful drawing!" or "You made a beautiful drawing!" or they gave no praise. Children with low self-esteem who heard the inflated praise ("incredibly beautiful") later opted to do more simple drawings, whereas kids with high self-esteem felt encouraged by the inflated praise to tackle more complicated drawings. On the other hand, the noninflated praise encouraged kids with low self-esteem to try the complicated drawings. Apparently low-key praise is easier for kids with low self-esteem to absorb, so they can feel encouraged without feeling pressured.

Teach How and Why to Accept Compliments

Kids with low self-esteem tend to respond to compliments by arguing. They say, "It wasn't that good" or "It was just luck" or "Jeremy did it better!" Maybe they think they're being modest, but what they're actually doing is insulting the judgment of the person giving them a compliment. Explain this to your child and role-play to practice graciously accepting a compliment by smiling and saying "Thank you." When kids are able to acknowledge a genuine compliment, they give themselves the opportunity to experience genuine pride.

Tell Empowering Stories

One of the most important ways that we influence our children is by the stories we help them create about themselves (McLean, Pasupathi, and Pals 2007). Telling stories about how your child struggled and then triumphed can contribute to creating a hopeful narrative and let her see beyond the current difficult situation.

Don't save these stories only for when your child is feeling sad or discouraged. Sprinkling them around at other times, when a relevant topic comes up, can help your child experience authentic pride. You could say something along the lines of "I remember when you were first learning to swim. You were afraid to put your face in the water! But you kept trying, and now you swim like a fish!"

Use the Language of Becoming

Ellen Wachtel (2001) offers another form of praise that can help children with low self-esteem change how they think about themselves and allow them to experience authentic pride. She calls it "the language of becoming." This involves noticing something that a child did and pairing that observation with a statement about how the child is becoming. Here are some examples:

"You stuck with that project, even though it was frustrating.

You are becoming good at persisting with hard work."

43

"You didn't react when your brother was teasing you.

You are becoming better able to keep your cool."

"You were kind to the new girl in your class by sitting with her at lunch.

You are becoming the kind of person who can make people feel welcome."

Hearing language of becoming is powerful for any child, but it's especially useful for children with low self-esteem because it allows them to see their identity as growing and evolving. It helps children to recognize progress instead of staying stuck in self-criticism. Past failings or future missteps recede in importance, as the language of becoming tells kids, *Here is evidence for hope!*

Beyond Praise and Criticism, Toward Intimacy

Correcting misbehavior and encouraging good behavior in our kids are necessary tasks in everyday parenting. How we go about doing these influences children's experience of self-conscious emotions, which over time contributes to their enduring view of themselves. But there's much more to raising our children than praise and criticism.

The most important part of parenting is the intimate connection we have with our children. Our deep acceptance of our children is a critical foundation for real self-esteem and helps fend off guilt and shame. When our children experience that we know, love, and value them *just as they are*, it's easier for them to let go of critical self-focus. Here are some ideas for fanning the flames of intimacy between you and your child.

Use the Power of Touch

One important way of connecting with kids is through touch. Touch can be comforting and soothing. It can communicate affection and even make children's positive emotions last longer (Bai, Repetti, and Sperling 2016). Some children are very open to hugs. Some like a cuddle or a back rub at bedtime. Some kids will only put up with a quick brush of their hair or squeeze of their shoulder, but even these brief touches can tell children, *You are precious to me!*

Know What Matters to Your Child

Get to know your child's friends. Let your child teach you about topics or activities that spark his interest. Play a conversation game together, such as TableTopics, which has intriguing and thought-provoking questions. Children are constantly changing. Maybe last year your daughter loved dolls, but now she's moved on. Maybe last month your son had never been on a skateboard, but now skateboarding is his passion. Your ongoing efforts to understand your child's shifting interests, with openness and curiosity, helps build closeness.

Reflect Feelings

Another simple but essential way of connecting with children is to reflect their feelings. Just describe the feelings that you see. When you, as a parent, acknowledge your child's emotions, you lighten the load of negative feelings and amplify positive ones. Reflecting feelings is important for all kids, but it's especially important for kids with low self-esteem because it communicates, *Your experience matters!* and *You matter to me!* This is a subtle but powerful counter-message to their sense of worthlessness.

Reflecting feelings doesn't come naturally to most parents. Here are some phrases you could use:

"You're feeling _____ because _____."

"It's hard for you when _____."

"It bothers you when _____."

"You wish _____."

Keep the emphasis on your child by saying "you feel" rather than "I understand." If you don't guess the feeling exactly right, that's okay. Your child will correct you. Either way, you and your child are doing the important work of wrapping feelings up in words and communicating them.

We're usually more comfortable acknowledging positive feelings: "You're so excited about that field trip!" "You really enjoy chocolate chip cookies!" It's harder to acknowledge negative feelings.

When our children experience negative feelings, our instinct is to go straight to a solution or to try to talk our kids out of distress: "Don't be discouraged!" "Don't worry. It'll be fine." "Quit complaining. It's not a big deal!" To spare our kids (and ourselves) from suffering, we immediately want to fix or brush past negativity. Unfortunately, this generally makes kids complain more and louder.

Suppose your child is saying, "I'm such a loser! I can't do anything right! Nothing good ever happens to me!" Obviously, you're not going to agree with these statements, but jumping in with counterarguments will just make your child more insistent. Your logical and well-intentioned arguments could make your child feel like you're not listening.

To avoid this no-win battle, reach for the feelings behind the complaints, and try to tie them to a particular situation or a specific time. For example, you could say, "You're feeling frustrated *by that project* because you're having trouble understanding *that one section*" or "You're feeling discouraged *right now* because you didn't play as well as you'd hoped *in that game*."

Unfortunately, your child is not going to respond to your reflection by saying, "Why, yes. What an insightful observation!" But you may get a grunt of acknowledgment or see a softening in your child's face or body. It may take several reflections before this happens. Don't try to move to problem solving until you see that softening. Even if you can't solve the problem, letting your child know that you hear what she is feeling can be a relief for your child. It means you're carrying part of the weight of that big problem.

Remember to Enjoy Your Child's Company

We're all busy. In the day-to-day rush of life, it's easy to become so focused on getting stuff done that we forget to enjoy spending time with our kids.

Enjoying your child's company doesn't have to involve elaborate trips to Disney. Those little connections, when you reunite after school or work or when you tuck them into bed, can be very precious moments of intimacy (Campos et al. 2009). Playing a game together, taking out your child for a one-on-one pizza date, and even cooking together can be easy ways to connect.

I don't have data on this, but from my experience as a clinician, I can tell you that laughing together is healing for kids with low self-esteem. It pulls them out of themselves and allows them to be in the moment.

Be careful about teasing, because kids with low self-esteem tend to be overly sensitive if they think anyone is laughing at them. You're on safer ground if you poke fun at yourself or just act silly. Do something ridiculous together. For instance, try this hilarious game: have all players fill their mouths with water, and then do whatever you can think of, short of physical contact, to try to make each other laugh. (This is definitely an outdoor sport!)

Plan Nondirective "Special" Time

If you want to use a more formal strategy for connecting, a play therapy approach that is part of parent-child interaction therapy can be useful for enhancing intimacy between parents and kids. This research-based approach has been found to increase a sense of closeness and security (even when parents and children are facing serious difficulties) with only five minutes a day of nondirective playtime (Urquiza and Timmer 2012).

So how do you do it? Invite your child to do some kind of non-competitive play with you. This could involve art supplies, building toys, or small figures. During this special playtime, offer no instructions, no criticism, and no questions. This is surprisingly hard to do!

47

We adults are just too used to poking at kids with "helpful" suggestions and reminders. To some extent, that's our job, but setting aside that directive role for a little while can have powerful effects on the sense of closeness between parents and kids.

Instead of directing the action, during this special playtime, try to be an admiring audience for your child. The acronym PRIDE describes your role in more detail:

P: Praise. Make positive (but not overblown) descriptive comments about what your child is doing. "You colored the whole thing very carefully!"

R: Reflect. Echo or paraphrase what your child says. "You like green."

I: Imitate. Copy what your child is doing (unless your child objects). "You're outlining everything before you color it in. I'm going to do that, too!"

D: Describe. Just say what your child is doing, as if you were a sports announcer, narrating the action. "You started with the left part, and now you're working on the right."

E: Express enthusiasm. "This is fun! I like watching you do that!" Keep the special playtime short, so you can do it regularly. It's likely to become one of your child's favorite activities, and you're also likely to relish this nondemanding time to enjoy your child's company.

Wrap-Up

Teaching our kids right from wrong is part of the job description of being a parent. But children with low self-esteem often react intensely to being corrected. They feel ashamed when they do something wrong and immediately jump to putting themselves down. When we respond gently to children's misbehavior, we help them experience healthy guilt rather than get trapped by paralyzing shame.

Beyond discipline, the moments of tenderness, understanding, and enjoyment you share with your child can diffuse harsh self-focus. The best compliment you can give your child, the one that best feeds real self-esteem, is "I enjoyed your company!"

The next chapter will look at sibling relationships, which can have a powerful effect on how children view themselves.

Take-Home Points

- Self-conscious emotions are feelings that stem from judgments of the self. These include shame, guilt, and pride.

- Low self-esteem results from inborn temperamental tendencies as well as life experiences.

- Kids with low self-esteem tend to see social feedback through a negative filter.

- Feelings of shame are linked to low self-esteem whereas feelings of guilt are not.

- Our connection with our kids is the foundation for real self-esteem.

"You Love Her More!"

When Your Child Struggles with Sibling Jealousy or Conflict

Chloe and her father sat at the kitchen table, going over flash cards. "What's the capital of Illinois?" he asked, holding up a flash card.

"Umm…Chicago?" Chloe guessed.

"I can't believe you don't know that!" Nathan scoffed at his sister. "We learned all the state capitals in second grade. How do you not know that in fourth grade?"

"Leave your sister alone," their father said wearily.

"Well, at least I got on the basketball team! You got cut in the first round!" Chloe retorted.

"That's cause you're a girl. It's easier to get on the girls' team. You're such a brat!" Nathan snapped back.

"Loser!"

"Brat!"

"Both of you, stop it!" their dad insisted.

"He started it!" Chloe said.

"Nathan, go to your room and do your homework. Chloe, come back here and finish doing these flash cards with me."

"It's not fair! You always take her side! You like her more!" Nathan yelled as he stormed off.

Ugh. Moments like these can make us parents wonder why we had kids in the first place.

Looking at this interaction through the lens of self-esteem, Nathan's opening salvo seems like a blatant attempt to build himself up by putting his sister down. Chloe, however, is no victim. Perhaps she feels ashamed of needing her dad's help to learn the state capitals, but she responds to her brother's taunting by going for the jugular. She brings up an incident that was probably very upsetting and even humiliating for her brother, asserting her own superiority. Poor, beleaguered Dad just wants the bickering to stop. Although he tries to be equitable and refocus both children on their homework, Nathan feels excluded and accuses his father of preferring his sister.

Sibling relationships tend to be intense and complicated. Brothers and sisters didn't choose to live together. They may share genes and a common home environment, but they can also be remarkably different. Siblings often have different interests, different personalities, and different styles of communicating...yet their connection to each other is likely to last longer than any other relationship.

When sibling relationships are hostile, competitive, or cruel, they can tear down children's self-esteem and create feelings of inadequacy. Because siblings know each other so well, arguments between them can devolve into vicious personal attacks that can be crushing for children with low self-esteem.

When sibling relationships are joyful, intimate, and supportive, they can offer a wonderful bedrock of *I've-seen-you-at-your-worst-and-I-love-you-anyway* connection that mutes self-criticism and promotes real self-esteem. For example, Clare Stocker (1994) interviewed second graders and found that compared to children with more difficult sibling relationships, those who reported greater warmth and less conflict with siblings also reported feeling less lonely and having better self-esteem. Caring siblings can also help kids learn how to interact with peers, compensate for a lack of friends, and be a source of comfort and security when families are facing stressful times (Milevsky 2016).

This chapter will focus on how siblings can affect children's self-esteem. We'll take a quick look at how family-structure characteristics, such as age, gender, and birth order, relate to sibling closeness. Then we'll look at dynamics within the family, focusing on sibling comparisons, jealousy, and conflict, and discuss what you as a parent can do about them.

Family Structure and Sibling Closeness

The constellation of sibling ages and genders that make up a particular family can have an impact on sibling relationships and (either directly or indirectly) on children's self-esteem (Milevsky 2016). However, exactly how family structure affects self-esteem can vary in different families. For instance, siblings who are similar in age may feel closer because they have more interests in common, which could provide self-esteem-bolstering acceptance, but they may also experience more rivalry and conflict, which could threaten self-esteem. The children in families with a greater number of siblings may have a group identity that leads to a sense of belonging, or they may have more conflict and competition over limited resources. The important thing is to consider how your particular family structure promotes or interferes with sibling closeness.

Closeness in Terms of Gender

There's some evidence that pairs of brothers tend to be less supportive and more aggressive than pairs of sisters (Buhrmester 1992). Parents of all-boy children report more family conflict than parents of all-girl children (Falconer, Wilson, and Falconer 1990). Brothers and sisters generally have more conflict and less intimacy than same-sex siblings, although there's often a jump in intimacy in relationships between brothers and sisters during the teen years, when they reach out to each other for dating advice (Kim et al. 2006). As kids move toward the teen years, they tend to argue less, but they're often less close, probably because they spend less time together.

Birth Order and Self-Esteem

Ideas about how birth order may affect self-esteem are popular but often contradictory. For instance, oldest siblings might have higher self-esteem because they get extra parental attention, or they might have lower self-esteem from having to contend with higher parental expectations and being dethroned when a sibling is born. Youngest siblings might have higher self-esteem because parents are less demanding and more nurturing toward the baby of the family, or they might have lower self-esteem because they get less individual attention and they're constantly outperformed by older siblings. Middle children might have low self-esteem from being sandwiched, neither as capable as the oldest nor as cute as the youngest, or their peacemaking abilities might make them the favored child. Large age gaps between siblings could also make the experience of a younger sibling more like that of an oldest or only child.

All of these scenarios seem plausible and likely to occur in some families, which may be why research findings about the effects of birth order and self-esteem tend to be contradictory. The largest, best-designed studies show no long-term link between birth order and personality (Damian and Roberts 2015).

Sibling Dynamics and Self-Esteem

Once children are born, the structure of a family in terms of sibling ages and spacing is set, but parents can influence the patterns of interaction between siblings. Sibling comparisons, jealousy, and conflict can have a powerful effect on children's self-esteem. The rest of this chapter will cover some tips for responding to these dynamics in ways that support both sibling closeness and real self-esteem.

Sibling Comparisons: Who's Better?

One way that children learn about who they are and what they can do is by comparing themselves to others. Siblings are handy gauges for these comparisons. Even two- to four-year-olds often compare themselves to their siblings in everyday conversation (Dunn and Kendrick 1982). How children believe they stack up relative to their brothers and sisters can lead to feelings of solidarity, superiority, or inadequacy—all of which are relevant for self-esteem.

Younger siblings often admire older siblings, especially same-sex older siblings, and want to be like them. They are most likely to try to copy a sibling they perceive as warm, caring, and similar to them but more powerful (Bandura 1962). Some older siblings enjoy being admired and imitated by their younger siblings (Davies 2011). However, when siblings are close in age, the older sibling is likely to feel annoyed and complain, "She's copying me!"

Siblings can be competitive with each other. This can range from fierce but playful striving to outdo each other in backyard-soccer games to bitter envy and even hatred triggered by a rival sibling's achievements (Volling, Kennedy, and Jackey 2010). Younger siblings have a readily available, face-saving excuse when an older sibling is more accomplished (*Well, she's older. I'll do better when I'm that age!*), but older siblings are likely to feel threatened by being out-performed by a younger brother or sister.

Together But Different

To minimize comparisons and protect their self-esteem, siblings sometimes deliberately or unconsciously choose to be different from one another. Psychologists call this *deidentification* or *differentiation*. For instance, if an older boy is a soccer star, his younger brother will probably choose a different interest to avoid having to live up to preestablished standards.

Unfortunately, sometimes children are too sweeping in their definition of a sibling's turf. While it doesn't matter if siblings have different tastes in music or if one sibling plays basketball and another plays soccer or the trumpet, it can be unduly limiting if one sibling (usually the younger) decides another sibling owns an entire area of expertise just because that sibling was there first. For instance, a child may not try at school, because a sister is good at academics.

Some siblings may feel a stronger need than others to establish their separate identities. In one study, Frances Schachter and her colleagues (1976) asked college students from families of three children whether they were similar to or different from their siblings. They found that 75 percent of the first pair of siblings (first and second child) in families saw themselves as different compared to 53 percent of the second pair (second and third child). Only 45 percent of the *jump pairs* (first and third child) saw themselves as different. First-pair siblings of the same sex were especially likely to see themselves as different.

Parents sometimes emphasize or even nudge children toward differentiating from siblings. In a study involving mothers' judgments of their two children, almost all mothers whose children were between ages six and fourteen reported that their two children were "different" or "opposite" (Schachter et al. 1978). (We'll talk more about family roles later in the chapter.)

Balancing Similarities and Differences

Family psychology theories emphasize *optimal differentiation*, which means having just the right amount of difference between siblings. Kids want to be similar enough have a sense of belonging, but they also want to be different enough to have a sense of individual identity.

On the basis of longitudinal data, clinical observation, and interviews with about one thousand brothers and sisters of various ages, Stephen Bank and Michael Kahn (2003) describe the major patterns of relationships between siblings as being on a continuum. At one extreme are relationships where siblings' perceptions of similarity eclipse their sense of self. This includes siblings who see themselves as so similar that they are almost the same person as well as relationships involving hero worship, where a younger sibling wants to become just like an older sibling. At the opposite extreme are relationships where perceptions of differences are so great that siblings feel completely disconnected. They don't like each other, don't depend on each other, and may not even care if they ever see each other.

In the middle are siblings who recognize that they are both alike and different. In the *healthy* version of this alike-and-different pattern, siblings feel connected by their similarities and accept their differences. In the *unhealthy* version of this pattern, siblings have what Bank and Kahn (2003) call a *hostile dependent* relationship. The siblings don't particularly like each other, but they are tied together by constantly trying to one-up the other. Their interactions are full of not-so-friendly put-downs and gloating. This pattern seems the most damaging for self-esteem because it intensifies comparison and self-judgment.

Taken all together, these research findings point to both the complexity of sibling relationships and their importance in how children view themselves. A sibling can be an ally, a rival, a mentor, an enemy, an intruder, a fan, or a relative stranger. What is certain is that when siblings grow up together, they can't help defining and measuring themselves, in some fashion, relative to each other. These comparisons can make children feel capable or inadequate and also influence children's relationships with their siblings.

Real Self-Esteem Tips to Try

Sibling comparisons can be a yardstick that children use to measure their worth. The one-dimensional question "Who's better?" can prompt anxious preoccupation with keeping score, but being a brother or a sister is not a winner-loser game. As parents, we can try to help siblings navigate the inevitable comparisons among themselves by supporting closeness without suffocation as well as uniqueness without disengagement. Here are some ideas about how to do this.

Never Compare Siblings Aloud

I'm sure you've noticed differences between your children. Don't say them aloud. Your kids already have a complicated job trying to figure out which similarities and differences they want to embrace, and your observations about differences could create unintended distance between them or trigger a self-fulfilling prophecy. Even positive comparisons can hurt. When parents say things like "You're good at science, and your sister is creative," they're trying to bolster each child's self-esteem by acknowledging unique areas of competence. Unfortunately, kids tend to hear these remarks as *Your sibling owns that area, and you're not allowed to venture near it!* This interpretation is quickly followed by their internal calculations about which area of competence is more desirable. Comments that divide realms of achievement between siblings also don't acknowledge areas of overlap (good scientists are creative!), and they fail to recognize that children are constantly changing. The differences that you observe today may not persist as your children grow and learn.

Identify Family Similarities and Values

A sense of belonging comes from having things in common with other people. What can you say is true about all members of your family? What are the interests, traits, habits, or values that bring you together? Have a discussion with your children to identify these. Maybe you're all curious people (even if you're interested in different topics), or you all care about the environment. Maybe you're all physically active (even if you enjoy different sports), or you're fans of a certain book series. Maybe it's favorite traditions that connect you, such as Saturday night movies and popcorn,. Having your children think about other families they know might help them figure out what it means to do things in your family way. You may want to record these observations in a list, a collage, or even a family mission statement. Figuring out the qualities that matter to your family can also help you find ways to make them an even bigger part of your daily life together.

Directly Challenge Overly Broad Turf Divisions

If you see your children assuming that certain activities are off-limits, just because a sibling excels in that area, you may need to confront the beliefs behind these restrictions. You could say something like, "Your brother doesn't own math!" and then express your confidence that your child can learn or become more capable in this area. You may want to use the analogy of teeth: some children lose their baby teeth early; some children do it later. All children end up with the right amount of adult teeth. Or, you could emphasize, "It's not where you start; it's whether you keep going!" to encourage your child not to give up. (See chapters 6 and 7.)

Encourage Older Siblings to Teach Younger Siblings

You don't want to overdo this and create resentment, but sometimes asking an older sibling to help a younger sibling learn a particular skill is a useful way to ease rivalry. Hiring the older sibling (perhaps for an affordable family rate of pay or a nonmonetary treat such as ice cream) acknowledges that child's expertise and allows the older child to enjoy a mature, helpful role. You may need to emphasize that the teaching has to be constructive and positive or that the older child only gets paid if the younger child has a good time. If things work out well, the older child will feel invested in— rather than threatened by—the younger child's success. The younger child will probably enjoy the attention and may be more willing to try, knowing that the older sibling will respond with encouragement rather than criticism.

Insist on Celebrating Sibling Successes

You may get some grumbling, but part of being a family involves cheering each other on. You could say to a grumpy sibling, "Yes, you do have to sit through his band concert, because it matters to him. Being supportive is the right thing to do." Kids sometimes need reminders to step beyond their own concerns. If showing support was difficult (maybe the band concert lasted a very long time), be sure to show appreciation. You may also want to give the supporting sibling a special job that contributes to the celebration. For instance, you could say, "I appreciate that you video-recorded your brother's solo and congratulated him on it. That was kind and generous of you." When the opportunity arises, make sure the other sibling reciprocates by showing interest and enthusiasm for this child's successes.

Sibling Jealousy: Who's the Favorite?

Another dynamic that can affect self-esteem is sibling jealousy, which reflects children's perceptions of how parents treat them versus their siblings. Sibling comparisons reflect concerns about *Who's better?* whereas sibling jealousy involves children's worries about *Who does Mom or Dad love more?* Children rarely mention competing for parents' attention or affection as a reason for sibling conflict (McGuire et al. 2000). However, they are acutely aware of when parents favor a sibling.

As early as one and two years of age, children carefully monitor their parents' interactions with a sibling (Dunn and Munn 1985). Older children can also readily describe times when they've felt jealous of a sibling. For example, Julie Thompson and Amy

Halberstadt (2008) asked fifth and sixth graders to describe sibling jealousy events. Their answers included when parents

1. Gave the sibling extra or better gifts.

2. Took the sibling's side in a conflict.

3. Spent more time with a sibling.

4. Or paid more attention to a sibling because of a special talent or ability.

Kids are on the lookout for parental favoritism, and they're keeping score!

What Research Tells Us About Parental Favoritism

Do parents really have favorite children? Apparently, a lot do. In one study, families with two parents and two children between nine and eighteen years old discussed various topics, while observers rated parents' negativity. Results showed that 70 percent of fathers and 74 percent of mothers directed more angry, hostile, or insensitive actions toward one child than the other (Shebloski, Conger, and Widaman 2005).

Probably every parent has found it easier or more enjoyable to be around one child than another at a certain stage or in a certain situation. My own children claim that my favorite child is whoever most recently washed the dishes. (True.) Transient moments of parental favoritism may elicit complaints from siblings, but they're unlikely to have significant impact on self-esteem. It's more concerning when a parent is frequently or consistently more critical and controlling with one sibling and more warm and affectionate toward the other.

Various studies have found links between parents' unequal treatment of siblings and more sibling conflict as well as lower self-esteem in the less-favored child (Meunier et al. 2012). What's not clear is whether being on the losing end of parental favoritism causes lower self-esteem or having low self-esteem leads kids to believe that their parents treat them unfairly, or whether some other variable, such as being anxious or impulsive, causes both low self-esteem and more negative interactions with parents.

The Trap of Treating Siblings Equally

Children are quick to complain, "No fair!" However, it's really not necessary or even desirable to treat our children equally, because children have different needs. A twelve-year-old shouldn't have the same bedtime as his six-year-old brother. One sibling, who tends to procrastinate, might need us to insist that she start her homework right away after school, but another sibling, who tends to be a perfectionist about homework, might need us to say that enough is enough.

However, we should pay attention to the meaning that kids attach to unequal parental treatment. It matters for both self-esteem and sibling harmony whether children believe that differences in parental treatment are fair and justified or are a sign that they are less lovable than their siblings (e.g., Kowal, Krull, and Kramer 2006).

Different family members don't necessarily view family interactions similarly. One child might consider a certain parental action to be unfair even if another child, the parent, or an objective observer doesn't see it that way. Children can sometimes have surprising interpretations of events. I know one family where the younger son needed a lot of parental attention and support because of a physical disability. Probably out of necessity, the older daughter was extremely independent and conscientious. One time, the daughter got a bad grade on a test because she'd been sick and missed a few days of school. The parents didn't give her a hard time about this, because they knew she was usually a very good student. But while the parents thought they were being understanding and supportive, their daughter was deeply hurt by their lack of concern about the bad grade. She interpreted the fact that they didn't scold or punish her as a sign that they didn't care what she did. Obviously, the answer was not to punish her but rather to give her room to talk about what it was like

61

to feel that she had to be the "easy" child of the family. She also needed to hear her parents express their love more directly and reassure her that they didn't expect her to be perfect.

Rigid Family Roles and Self-Esteem

This brings us to a very important topic related to sibling jealousy and self-esteem. While no parent is ever going to be perfectly fair, in some families, due to a combination of circumstances and personal characteristics, children get trapped in a rigid role within the family that sets them apart from their siblings. Rigid roles can take many forms, but their key feature is that they box kids into behaving a certain way that interferes with their own growth and hurts their relationships with other family members.

One example of this kind of role is the *bad kid* of the family. This child isn't really bad, of course, but he or she might be especially determined, energetic, intensely emotional, or just going through a challenging developmental stage. This leads to the child getting in trouble noticeably more than other kids in the family. Eventually, it becomes this child's job within the family to cause trouble. That's what everyone expects, so the child gives up trying to be any other way. The bad-kid role is often counterbalanced within a family with an equally restrictive good-kid role for a sibling who believes he or she has to be perfect to make up for the challenges of the bad kid.

Another example of a rigid role is what's called the *parentified child*. Maybe because parents are overwhelmed, this child gets pushed into overly grown-up responsibilities, such as frequently being in charge of younger siblings. This creates resentment among siblings and can be overwhelming for the parentified child.

A third example of a rigid family role is the child who is put in the role of a parent's *special buddy*. It's common for parents to feel they are more similar to or have more in common with one child in the family, but when the special-buddy role becomes rigid, it's often a symptom of marital conflict. While being the chosen one might feel exciting for a child, it can lead to distance and resentment from the other parent and siblings. Also, the child may feel guilty about having the privileged role or be anxious about losing it. If the parent remarries, the special-buddy child is likely to get demoted, which can be baffling and upsetting.

If you see your children falling into rigid roles, help them break out of these by noticing, encouraging, and even creating opportunities for them to interact with family members in ways that don't fit their role. This could include giving the "bad" kid the chance to do something responsible or nurturing, the "good" kid a chance to be silly, the parentified child to be taken care of, or the special buddy to spend time doing something fun with the other parent.

More Real Self-Esteem Tips to Try

Feeling jealous of a sibling can get in the way of closeness between siblings and also prompt negative self-judgments as children try to explain to themselves why their parents seem to prefer a sibling. Here are some ways to address your child's concerns about favoritism.

Address the Real Issue Behind Sibling Jealousy

When kids accuse parents of favoritism, parents are often tempted to reassure them by saying they love all of their children equally. This is not at all satisfying! None of us wants to be loved equally; we each want to be loved specially. So when your child complains that you love a sibling more, don't fall into the trap of debating fairness or trying to seem impartial. Instead, give your child a hug and say something like, "You are the only one I love in a special Timmy way!" Then list the sweet qualities that you love about your child, emphasizing ones that don't have to be earned. You could say, "I love the way you giggle at knock-knock jokes. I love the way you're so gentle with your little cousin. I love the way you're always interested in looking at the weather map when there's a storm. I love kissing that sweet spot at the back of your neck…"

Spend Enjoyable One-on-One Time with Each Child

Having Mom or Dad all to themselves for a while is fun for kids and builds self-esteem-supporting connection. Keep the activity simple, so you can do it again soon. You may want to make it a regularly scheduled event.

Don't Fuss Over Making Everything Exactly Equal

If we anxiously count the number of sprinkles on each child's cupcake, we communicate to our kids that minor inequalities are dangerous and unbearable. We teach them that they, too, should be vigilant about checking to make sure everything is exactly equal. This is annoying and probably impossible. It creates a self-absorbed *What do I get?* view of relationships that is incompatible with the outward focus of real self-esteem.

Certainly, you don't want to deliberately and arbitrarily create gross injustices between siblings, but you also don't have to scramble to make up for every little perceived slight. It may help to acknowledge your child's frustration or disappointment. You could say, "You're feeling frustrated because he got to do that, and you couldn't" or "It bothers you that you had to do it, and she didn't." And you can follow that up by offering a hug and saying, "Sometimes things aren't fair. You're strong enough to handle that."

Be Open to Changing How You Do Things

Sometimes children raise valid points about unfairness that deserve to be addressed. Maybe your child has grown up some, and the old rules or procedures no longer make sense. Maybe you just weren't aware of how something came across to that particular child, and you didn't mean it that way. Being heard is empowering for children. So, while we don't want to make our whole lives revolve around ensuring fairness between siblings, we do want to be responsive to genuine concerns.

Think About Your Own Family Patterns Growing Up

Our own experiences growing up can lead to special sensitivities or blind spots that influence how we perceive our kids' interactions. For instance, if your parents let your younger sister get away with murder, you may tend to side with your older child. If you were bullied by an older brother, you may overreact to the slightest sign of bossiness from your eldest child. Being aware of how old family patterns shaped us can help us temper our automatic reactions, so we can respond more thoughtfully and perhaps more kindly or fairly to our children.

Sibling Conflict

The third family dynamic that can affect self-esteem is sibling conflict. By far, the biggest concern parents tend to have about siblings is the frequency and intensity of their arguing. When sibling conflict gets out of control, it can undermine self-esteem-supporting closeness between siblings. The last part of this chapter will cover research on sibling conflict as well as the best ways parents can respond to these squabbles.

Arguments between siblings are extremely common. In one study, Laurie Kramer and her colleagues (1999) recorded pairs of siblings between three and nine years of age playing together in their own homes. The children averaged a bit more than five conflicts across a total of ninety minutes of observation. That works out to about one disagreement every eighteen minutes. So, if you feel like your kids are at each other all the time, that's because sometimes they really are!

There are huge differences in how siblings get along. Researchers classify sibling relationships into four main patterns:

1. Low conflict plus high warmth is the pattern that parents wish for.

2. High conflict plus low warmth is the most painful pattern.

3. Low conflict plus low warmth is peaceful, but siblings are disengaged.

4. High conflict and high warmth—which means that the arguments are balanced by fun and kindness—is the most common pattern.

Surprisingly, the last pattern, with both a lot of conflict and a lot of warmth, is the one that elementary school children rate as most satisfying (McGuire, McHale, and Updegraff 1996). In terms of connection that supports children's self-esteem, sibling warmth matters more than conflict.

Characteristics of Sibling Conflicts

Siblings argue most frequently over *objects* or *physical space* (Howe, Ross, and Recchia 2011). This includes those enthralling debates along the lines of "That's my sweater!" and "I was here first!" Next most frequently, they argue over *activities*, such as "You always get to pick the game!" or "You went first last time!" followed by accusations that the sibling is being annoying. You've probably heard all of these.

Although we adults tend to believe that children's conflicts should be resolved through reasonable compromise, research tells us that the majority of sibling conflicts don't get resolved in fair and happy ways. In one study involving pairs of siblings between three and ten years old, only about 12 percent of conflicts were resolved through compromise, whereas 77 percent had win-lose outcomes, mostly in favor of the older sibling (Abuhatoum and Howe 2013).

However, if we give siblings a chance to talk things over at a later point in time, removed from the heat of the argument, they can reach a compromise about half the time (Howe, Ross, Recchia 2011). Siblings will also do better problem solving if they focus on the future rather than just rehash past wrongs (Ross et al. 2006). Resolving conflicts with siblings can encourage self-esteem-supporting connection and also prepare children to deal with conflicts with peers.

While siblings are growing up, the older child is likely to be more bossy and aggressive than the younger, but older siblings can also play an important role in teaching or caring for younger siblings and coming up with fun play ideas. Also, younger siblings aren't helpless. They quickly learn to yell or to bring parents in to defend them. Younger siblings are also more likely to invoke family rules or principles of fairness to bolster their position (Abuhatoum and Howe 2013). As children get older, they become more equal both physically and verbally.

An important thing to remember is that siblings generally get along better when *parents* get along better (Kim et al. 2006). Intense or frequent conflict between parents is stressful for kids, and it also teaches them how to be nasty to each other. Both open warfare and enduring silent resentment between parents is harmful for children. If our goal is to promote real self-esteem by having siblings be a source of support for each other, we have to start by being good examples of kindness and connection.

When Siblings Resort to Cruelty

Sibling conflicts can get very heated and sometimes even violent. One survey found that over a period of one year, 70 percent of families reported physical violence of some sort between siblings, and over 40 percent of children were kicked, bitten, or punched by a sibling (Straus, Gelles, and Steinmetz 1981). Another national survey found that 45 percent of two- to nine-years olds and 36 percent of ten- to thirteen-year-olds had experienced at least one incident of sibling aggression in the past year (Tucker et al. 2013). Fortunately, the vast majority of these incidents didn't result in injury.

Even without physical violence, siblings can be vicious to each other. Holly Recchia and her colleagues (2013) interviewed seven-, eleven-, and sixteen-year-old children about times they had hurt a younger sibling or a friend. The children described hurting friends as being unusual and unforeseeable occurrences, but they described hurting a sibling as a typical, ruthless, and provoked action. There was a tone of casual cruelty and self-justification to these stories. For instance, a seven-year-old boy remarked, "Ben was making faces at me, and I'm not really good at faces. I'm actually really good with my hands…and I hit him." An eleven-year-old girl reported, "I called him a stupid, mean, nasty little elf-brother! He *is* pretty short." Although the children did say they felt remorseful about hurting their sibling, nastiness like this can't be helpful for either their relationship with their sibling or their sibling's self-esteem, and it may even hurt the older siblings' self-esteem by making them feel guilty or ashamed of their mean behavior.

How Parents Usually Respond

Observational research shows that about half of the time, parents ignore sibling conflicts to give kids a chance to work things out on their own, but parents also report that they don't believe that ignoring conflicts is a particularly effective strategy (Kramer, Perozynski and Chung 1999). When parents ignore sibling battles, siblings may take this as permission to carry on and argue even more forcefully.

If they do get involved in sibling conflicts, parents tend to act like a judge, pronouncing a verdict to settle the matter. Unfortunately, if a parent approaches two battling siblings, both will try to convince the parent to be on their side. When parents get involved in this way, it encourages kids to tattle and to immediately seek parent backing by arguing their case rather than trying to work things out on their own.

Even More Real Self-Esteem Tips to Try

Sibling conflict is important to address, especially when it gets vicious, because it can undermine children's self-esteem. Serious and prolonged abuse from a sibling can lead children to conclude that no one cares if they're hurt, that they're helpless to stop it, or even that they deserve to be hurt. Although we don't want to have to deal with every little squabble between siblings, we also can't permit conflicts to escalate into cruelty or all-out warfare.

Here are some ideas for addressing sibling conflicts to minimize cruelty and help bolster the closeness between your children that supports real self-esteem.

Ignore Minor Arguments

Not every issue between siblings has to be settled with United Nations–worthy diplomacy and justice. Give your kids room to try to work out small issues by themselves. Feel free to ignore mild squabbling with no real heat behind it.

If you want to encourage better resolutions, try just stating a general expectation, such as "What would be fair to both of you?" Then get out of the room.

If sibling bickering is getting on your nerves, you could try bursting into a lively rendition of a song about peace. There are many: "Let There Be Peace on Earth," "Give Peace a Chance," "Peace is Flowing Like a River." Your performance will convey a family value—and probably clear the room.

Stop or Prevent Real Cruelty

Draw the line at behavior between siblings that is physically damaging, destructive, truly vicious, or humiliating. Most of the time, when things are very heated, your best bet is to say, "Both of you go to your room. It's not safe for you to be together right now." If needed, you can add, "We'll talk about this later, when everyone is feeling calmer."

Challenge Rationalizations for Meanness

Explain to your kids that rationalizations are excuses for behaviors that we know are wrong. Examples include: "I was just kidding," "He did it first," "She made me do it," and "They did something worse." None of those excuses make meanness acceptable.

Mediate Serious or Repeated Problems

Kids aren't born knowing how to solve relationship problems. It takes effort and practice to learn to consider someone else's perspective. As a mediator, you can guide your children toward coming up with their own solution. Give each child a chance to explain his or her side, have each child acknowledge the other's concerns, and then encourage your kids to suggest and evaluate possible solutions. It might be tempting to just blurt out the answer for them, but the process of struggling to find a solution offers useful learning. Mediation takes time, so you'll probably want to save it for important or recurrring problems. The more you do it, the faster your kids will get at it, and the better equipped they'll be to do it on their own.

Encourage Sibling Fun and Unity

Having fun together builds warmth and caring between siblings. It also motivates them to treat each other with kindness and to resolve problems peacefully. Encourage your kids to do a project together. Or, try playing a kids-versus-the-grown-ups game with them, to help your children see each other as allies. Activities or outings involving the whole family can also build cohesiveness.

Wrap-Up

Sibling relationships are complicated. A sibling can be a standard by which children define or measure themselves, a rival for parental attention, or a lifelong buddy and source of support. When children are preoccupied with feeling somehow less worthy than their siblings, it can contribute to low self-esteem. On the other hand, when children know that their siblings have their back, even if they squabble sometimes, it can move them toward real self-esteem.

When you decided to have more than one child, you probably had fantasies of them being best friends forever. That might happen! Although research and daily experience showing how frequently siblings argue can be dismaying, conflict doesn't necessarily prevent closeness. Helping siblings embrace their similarities as well as their differences, refrain from nit-picking about fairness, avoid rigid family roles, minimize meanness, and have fun together paves the way for them to cultivate a sense of belonging that supports real self-esteem.

The final chapter in this section on connection will turn to children's friendships. It will look at how peer relationships affect self-esteem and how you can help your child learn to make and keep friends.

Take-Home Points

- Children's self-esteem can be affected by patterns of interactions with siblings, such as comparisons, jealousy, and conflict.

- How children believe they stack up relative to their brothers and sisters can lead to feelings of solidarity, superiority, or inadequacy—all of which are relevant to self-esteem.

- Studies have found links between parents' unequal treatment of siblings and more sibling conflict as well as lower self-esteem in the less-favored child.

- Rigid family roles for children (such as bad kid, good kid, parentified child) box them in and hurt their relationships with siblings.

- When sibling conflict gets out of control, it can undermine the closeness between siblings that supports real self-esteem.

"Nobody Likes Me!"

When Your Child Feels Friendless

Marissa walked into the house, dropped her backpack, and slumped down on the chair.

"What's wrong, Sweetie?" her mom asked.

"Everything!" Marissa groaned. "Today, Cece spent all of recess playing with Samantha. Ayami and Laura were playing together, and Francine and the other girls were doing four square, which I hate, so I was all by myself."

"Well, I'm sure some of those girls would have included you if you'd asked."

"No, they wouldn't have. Everybody has a best friend except me. Nobody likes me. They always leave me out!"

●

Marissa's low self-esteem is tied to feeling rejected by the other girls. Although no one is being overtly mean to her, she sees everyone else paired up, which leaves her feeling like an outsider.

But is Marissa really being rejected by the other girls? That's hard to say. Research on rejection sensitivity shows that some people are especially prone to seeing rejection, even when it's not intended (McLachlan, Zimmer-Gembeck, and McGregor 2010). Past experiences of being rejected can lead kids to have anxious or angry expectations that peers will reject them again and to be quick to interpret even neutral events as signs of rejection. The other girls were playing different games with different people that day, but, as Marissa's mom suggests, maybe they were open to including Marissa. On the other hand, maybe Marissa is doing something that makes other kids less willing to play with her.

This chapter will look at ways to help children develop satisfying friendships and a sense of connection that quiets negative self-focus.

Friendship Matters

Friendship is extremely important for children. Friends are a source of fun and belonging. Having friends helps children discover who they are outside the family. Friends also help children deal with difficulties. When kids have even one friend who likes them back, they have higher self-esteem, feel less lonely, have more positive attitudes toward school, are less likely to be bullied, and cope better with stressful events (Bukowski et al 2009).

On the flip side, children who are widely rejected by their peers often struggle with feelings of loneliness and inadequacy.

One theory of self-esteem, called *sociometer theory*, says that self-esteem serves as an internal barometer informing us how accepted we are by a group (Leary and Baumeister 2000). Because humans need others to survive, from an evolutionary perspective, it's useful to feel uncomfortable when we're sensing that we're on the outside of a group.

Theoretically, the pinch of feeling rejected can motivate kids to behave in ways that will put them back in the good graces of the group. Practically, as a clinician, I can tell you that kids with low self-esteem often respond to feeling rejected—or the possibility of being rejected—in ways that cause the rejection to continue or even increase! They focus on their *own* feelings of hurt, anxiety, or discomfort, they pick apart their social performance, or they withdraw from interacting with other kids. All of this gets in the way of their creating or maintaining satisfying friendships.

Sociometric Status

Researchers have spent a lot of time investigating how children do or don't fit in with their peers. In a typical study, all of the children in a certain grade at school report which three kids in their grade they like best and which three they like least. Based on these reports, researchers determine what they call *sociometric status* by classifying kids into five groups (e.g. Cillessen and Mayeux 2004b):

Most kids fall into the *average* group, which means they don't stand out, because they get a medium amount of both likes and dislikes.

Well-liked children get lots of likes and few dislikes. These kids tend to be friendly, cooperative, and kind. They can be assertive when they need to be, but they don't get involved in a lot of conflict.

Controversial children are a mixed bag. They get a lot of likes and a lot of dislikes. They are often social leaders who set their own rules. They may be kind to friends and not so kind to other kids.

Neglected children fly under the radar. They get few likes and few dislikes. These children tend to have a quieter style of interacting. They are often well-liked by teachers. Over time, as their peers get to know them better, they tend to move into other groups.

Rejected children get lots of dislikes and few likes. These are the kids we worry about most.

Why Some Kids Are Rejected

Researchers have looked at the behavior of rejected children and found that there are several subtypes. Many rejected children have angry outbursts that are scary or off-putting for their peers. Rejected boys tend to get into physical fights, while rejected girls are more likely to make bossy or harshly critical remarks. Sometimes peers deliberately try to provoke rejected kids for entertainment. Unfortunately, when the rejected kids explode in response to taunting, they further separate themselves from other kids.

Some rejected kids cry a lot in public. Whenever they feel frustrated or slighted, they burst into tears. While this might get some sympathy from peers initially, if it happens too frequently, other kids are likely to ignore or avoid them or even mock them for being "babyish." From about first grade on, there is a social cost to crying in public. Also, children who spend a lot of time crying are spending less time playing, learning, talking, and doing other fun and interesting things that support friendships.

Still other rejected kids are anxious and withdrawn. They keep themselves apart from their peers, not showing or responding to friendly gestures.

Finally, some rejected children are out of sync with their peers. They may have interests that their peers consider peculiar or babyish, they may have unusual and off-putting habits, or they may have poor hygiene. The hygiene problem is the most easily remedied! With kids who tend to resist taking showers, changing into clean clothes in the morning, or brushing their teeth, you may want to give them a sniff before they head off to school and have them "try again" if they don't pass the smell test.

Sociometric Status and Friendship

Sociometric status isn't the same as friendship, but it's related. Sociometric status reflects kids' *general reputation*; friendship involves *particular relationships*. In a study by Scott Gest and his colleagues, involving seven- and eight-year-olds, almost a third of children who were generally well-liked by their peers said they didn't have a friend (Gest, Graham-Berhmann, and Hartup 2001). This means that a good reputation doesn't guarantee having friends, but kids who are generally well-liked certainly have an easier time making friends than kids who are widely disliked.

At the other end of the sociometric spectrum, Gest found that 39 percent of the rejected children *did* have a reciprocated friendship. However, the friendships that rejected children have tend to be less enjoyable and satisfying than those of other kids. Poorer quality friendships are less supportive and more conflict-ridden. It's not clear whether rejected kids are settling for poorer quality friendships because they don't have other options or because they don't know how to build and maintain high-quality friendships.

Real Self-Esteem Tips to Try

So how can we help children like Marissa? Marissa's insistence that "Nobody likes me" doesn't help her move forward. It keeps her trapped in the low-self-esteem whirlpool of feelings of hurt and inadequacy. Instead of dwelling on feeling rejected, Marissa needs to shift to thinking about *What can I offer and to whom?* This doesn't mean turning into a spineless people-pleaser; it does mean letting go enough of self-focus to be able to care about others.

With children whose low self-esteem is related to friendship issues, we need to help them build real connections with their peers by *moving toward a generous, outward focus.* This means (1) avoiding off-putting behaviors and (2) building connections.

Address Off-Putting Behaviors

Almost all kids face friendship problems of some sort, at some time, but kids with low self-esteem are quick to see these as a sign of personal inadequacy and a permanent state. They think they're not smart enough, not cool enough, or just plain not likable enough, and that's what makes everyone reject them. But they're often blind to things they do that push others away, because they're focused on how they are feeling rather than how they are affecting others.

Teach Self-Calming to Prevent Big Emotional Displays

Big emotional displays, whether anger or tears, are uncomfortable for other kids to be around. Of course, kids are allowed to feel whatever they feel, but they also need to learn to manage their feelings so they don't become overwhelmed by them.

A young girl once told me, "I know how to make friends. I just sit at the edge of the playground and look very sad, so people feel bad for me and come over."

This is not a good friendship strategy! It might work once, but pretty soon the other kids are likely to decide that they'd rather play with classmates who are happy and having fun. This girl was focused on her own feelings, not on connecting with her peers.

Practicing calming strategies such as slow breathing (breathe out for a count of four, breathe in for a count of four), doing mental arithmetic (adding or subtracting by threes or sevens), or just noticing shapes in the floor tiles can help kids tolerate distress. Using silent coping statements that they've prepared and rehearsed in advance, such as *I don't like this, but I can handle it* or *I'm strong enough to deal with this*, can help kids stay anchored during a challenging situation.

If they still feel overwhelmed, they may need to step away from the situation temporarily by taking a short break or a quick trip to the bathroom to settle themselves. During this break, they should refrain from going over and over in their minds how terrible the situation is and how wronged they are, because that will only increase their distress. Instead, they should use their coping strategies or distract themselves, so they can calm down enough to think and come up with some ideas about how to handle the situation.

Encourage Problem Solving Instead of Tattling

Disagreements with peers are unavoidable. In addition to learning how to calm themselves, kids need ideas of what to do when they have a conflict with a peer. For many kids with low self-esteem, because they are so focused on their own distress, tattling is their go-to coping strategy for dealing with any problem. While this might get teacher intervention, it certainly won't win points with other kids. (If it happens too often, it can also be annoying to teachers.) Starting around first grade, kids need to avoid publicly tattling on other kids. When older elementary school and middle school kids tattle, they invite very strong disapproval from their peers. The tattling comes across as mean and babyish.

If there is a serious ongoing situation that requires adult intervention, such as severe or persistent bullying, it's best if kids tell an adult discreetly, at a later time, when other kids aren't around. They definitely shouldn't announce to peers, "I'm telling!"

Kids may need to plan, during a calm moment, how to handle challenging situations that come up repeatedly. Sometimes the right answer is to speak up directly to the other kid. For instance, your child could say, "I had that first," "It's my turn," "I was the frog last time. This time I want to be something else," or "The way we're dividing the work on this project doesn't seem fair to me. I think we should all help with the references."

This type of direct communication is very different from helpless self-focus. Rather than stewing with resentment or angrily accusing other kids of being mean, these matter-of-fact statements empower kids to communicate their wants or needs in a respectful way that others can hear. For many kids, it takes practice to learn how to be assertive. You may want to try role-playing with your child saying calm and direct statements in different scenarios.

Yelling, name-calling, and accusations don't invite positive responses! Assertive statements emphasize I ("I think..." "I want...") rather than you ("You are..." "You always..." "You never..."). Also, it's usually best to describe what the speaker wants to happen rather than just tell someone to stop. For example, "I'm feeling crowded. Please move over" is easier to hear and more respectful than "Stop being annoying!"

To practice assertive responses with your child, you can role-play actual situations that your child has encountered or try some of the ones listed below. What could your child say that both is respect-ful of the other person and addresses your child's wants and needs? Keep in mind that tone of voice and body language matter even more than what your child says. Assertive words said in an angry or overly meek and tentative way won't work to get your child's message across. Here are some examples:

1. *Jeremy took your pencil.*

   Possible assertive response: "That's my pencil. I need it back, please."

2. *Caroline cut in front of you in line.*

   Possible assertive response: "Excuse me, I was waiting here first. Please go to the back of the line."

3. *Amrit keeps calling you an annoying nickname.*

   Possible assertive response: "I don't like it when you call me that. Please use my real name."

4. *Maria and Priya keep taking and hiding your cookies at lunch.*

   Possible assertive response: "This isn't fun for me. Please give me back my cookies."

Assertiveness isn't always the right answer. Some kids are not open to hearing what your child thinks or feels, so it may not make sense to try to be assertive with them. Staying away from these peers as much as possible may be the best option. Even with kids who are usually friendly, when there's a big disagreement, it may be best to just move away and hang out with someone else for a while to let tempers cool. We adults tend to want to talk everything out, but that's not what kids usually do. Observational research shows that many children's conflicts are resolved by kids taking a short break from each other (for as little as a few minutes or sometimes for the rest of the day) and then reconnecting just by acting kind or friendly (Verbeek, Hartup, and Collins 2000).

Discourage Possessiveness

Sometimes when kids with low self-esteem have a friend, they desperately cling to that friend so much that the friend feels strangled. This is another example of focusing on their own insecurity at the expense of being aware of someone else's feelings. Kids with low self-esteem are acutely aware of their own desperate desire to have a friend and their fear of being alone, which may cause them to overlook their friend's feelings.

While it's important to reach out to friends, it's also important to give friends a chance to reciprocate, so that the friendship doesn't feel like a pursuit. Friendship should be like a game of catch: one person throws the ball, and the other person catches it and throws it back, alternating back and forth.

What does this look like practically? A good rule of thumb is that if your child invites a friend over, she should wait at least two weeks before offering another invitation. This way, the friend has a chance to reach out and won't feel bombarded by invitations.

A very challenging situation for kids is when a friend has another friend. They often feel jealous or betrayed when their friend wants to spend time with someone else. Forcing a friend to choose between them and a rival is a good way to drive that friend away. Trying to divide the friend's time ("You can sit with her on Mondays and Wednesdays, and you have to sit with me on Tuesdays and Thursdays...") also doesn't work, because it feels too controlling. Instead, kids need to have compassion for their friend and do their best to cultivate a good relationship with the other child. If they are not rivals, then the friend doesn't have to choose one side or the other.

Trying to expand a friendship to include a rival doesn't always work, but it's the best option. Possessiveness is pretty much guaranteed to end friendships. The tighter kids try to hold a friend, the more the friend will want to get away.

Help Your Child Build Connections

Making friends requires more than just avoiding off-putting behaviors. Kids also need to reach out to build genuine connections. Again, focusing on others—rather than getting tangled up with their own fears—will help kids with low self-esteem do this.

Start with Hello

Kids with low self-esteem often struggle with the first few seconds of interaction. They see someone they know or someone says hello to them, and they just sink in on themselves, drawing up their shoulders, avoiding eye contact, and turning away. Feelings of awkwardness and self-consciousness are behind this withdrawal, but the message these behaviors send to other kids is *I don't like you, and I don't want anything to do with you!*

If your child has trouble with greetings, you may want to start by having your child observe how and how often other children greet each other. For instance, your child could count how many greetings he hears at the start of a school day. Becoming aware of how common greetings are can help your child become more open to giving them. Kids worry that greeting someone will draw unwanted attention, but it's the nongreeting that stands out—and not in a good way!

Next, help your child practice giving friendly greetings. This involves smiling, making eye contact and speaking loudly enough that the other person hears. If your child feels uncomfortable making eye contact, here's a good trick: look people in the forehead. Have your child focus on the area between the other person's eyebrows. No one will know your child isn't really making eye contact.

Whenever possible, it's also a good idea to say the other person's name because that makes the greeting more personal. Explain to your child that a greeting tells someone, *I'm happy to see you!* Your child can begin practicing greetings with family members in the morning and again when reuniting in the afternoon or evening. You could even make it a contest to see if your child can greet you before you greet her!

Once your child is used to greeting family members, it's time to try greeting peers. You may want to set a goal with your child of how many kids to greet each day. Some children need to start by just trying to greet one person each day in a friendly way. That's fine. With practice, greeting others will become easier and feel more natural.

Try to Connect Rather Than Impress

One of the things that can make social interactions very stressful for kids with low self-esteem is that they often believe that they have to be impressive to make friends. The most minor interaction feels like a performance in front of a critical audience. Before getting together with a peer, they worry that they'll do something wrong. During the interaction, they feel unbearably anxious if they don't know exactly what to do or how to respond. Afterward, they pick apart every little thing they said or did, magnifying mistakes and imagining others' scorn.

All of this self-focus heightens kids' anxiety, increases their sense of inadequacy, and gets in the way of friendly, comfortable interaction. Plus it's exhausting! No wonder so many kids with low self-esteem avoid getting together with potential friends. Unfortunately, avoiding social interactions makes them feel even more uncomfortable around peers.

To break out of this cycle, kids need to understand: *The spotlight is not on you!* Trying to impress others won't help children make or keep friends. A better strategy is for children to focus on helping the other person feel comfortable and liked. Instead of trying to perform exceptionally well—which would make anyone feel self-conscious— all they need to do is be kind and show interest in the other person. This is much easier than trying to be amazing!

There are hundreds of small ways children can be kind:

- Smile at someone.

- Give someone a sincere compliment ("Nice catch!" or "Your project looks cool!").

- Ask *what* and *how* questions to get to know someone better ("What do you think of the new movie?" or "How was your weekend?").

- Offer to share ("Here, you can borrow my pencil" or "I have extra paper. Do you want some?").

- Invite someone to join ("You can sit here. There's room!" or "Do you want to be partners for the dinosaur diorama?").

See if your child can come up with more ideas. To encourage acts of kindness, you may want to help your child record them in a journal or have every family member report their acts of kindness that day at dinnertime.

Some kids overdo kindness by giving away money, food, or prized possessions. Acts that leave your child feeling sad and resentful will *not* help build friendships. They also won't make other kids like your child more. Friendships have to be gently cultivated; they can't be bought.

Build on Common Ground

Sometimes kids feel friendless because they're targeting the wrong people. Not everyone is open to friendship with them. From preschool onwards, children show preferences for playing with certain peers more than others. Some children become hyperfocused on one particular child who doesn't like them. This is a recipe for misery.

Sometimes the reason children want to be friends with a certain peer is because that child is popular. In later elementary school and middle school, social hierarchies emerge with some kids being more socially dominant than others. These popular kids are not necessarily kind or trustworthy, but they are socially powerful, and everyone seems to want to be their friend. One study found that fewer than one-third of children who are described by their peers as popular are also well-liked (Parkhurst and Hopmeyer 1998).

Popular kids tend to be especially athletic, attractive, or wealthy (Adler and Adler 1995). Some of these children use ridicule, gossip, and exclusion to maintain their social prominence. They may enjoy having lower-status kids seek their attention, and they may dole out enough approval to keep their fans hooked, but they won't befriend kids whom they see as beneath them. That would lessen their social cachet. Begging for crumbs from popular kids is a soul-destroying social role!

Rather than striving to befriend the most popular kid in school, your child will do better to build friendships based on common ground. A robust finding from research is that children tend to befriend children who are similar to them (Rubin et al 2015). The most important similarity is what they like to do. *Kids make friends by doing fun things together.* If children have little or nothing in common, they are unlikely to become friends or stay friends.

Have your child identify favorite activities. These interests could lead naturally to a friendship. For instance, if your child enjoys basketball, she could invite a teammate to go out for ice cream after practice. If he enjoys reading, he could chat about favorite books at lunch with a classmate who also likes to read. If your child can't think of any activities to share with others, you may need to nudge your child into trying some new activities that could lead to friendships. You may want to offer two choices that you think your child might enjoy and insist that your child pick one of these or come up with a good alternative.

Watch, Then Blend

For children, individual friendships often begin within the context of a group. But kids with low self-esteem tend to hold themselves apart from their peers. They watch other kids having fun but don't participate. Sometimes they believe they aren't allowed to join in unless they are specifically invited to do so. A would-you-be-so-kind-as-to-join-us invitation rarely happens among children. Unfortunately, kids with low self-esteem tend to interpret the lack of this kind of red-carpet invitation as *They don't want anything to do with me!* More likely, the other kids are just too busy having fun to stop and notice who else might want to be included.

Sometimes kids with low self-esteem are afraid to approach groups because they're worried that other kids will publicly reject and humiliate them. Fortunately, kids don't have to make a big announcement to join a group. In fact, research involving observations of kids on playgrounds tells us that the children who are successful in joining groups at play usually *don't* draw attention to themselves. Instead, they watch what the other kids are doing and then slide into the action without interrupting (Dodge et al 1983).

For instance, if the other kids are playing tag, your child can watch to see who is "It" and then start running around near the tagger. If the other kids are playing kickball, your child could retrieve a ball that goes out of bounds, then stand in line to join the losing team. If kids are lining up to pick teams or play a game, your child should hurry over to line up, too.

Have your child list some of the activities that kids often do at recess. Which groups would be easiest to join? Plan together some ways that your child could watch then blend.

It's usually not a good idea to ask, "Can I play?" This draws attention to your child and interrupts the game. The other kids have to stop what they're doing, turn around, look at your child, and decide whether they want your child to join. This is disrespectful of their game, and it also provides too much of an opportunity for a mischievous kid to say, "No! Hah hah!"

Research also tells us that kids are more likely to be successful joining a single child at play or a group of four or more (Putallaz and Wasserman 1989). Twosomes and threesomes may be too tight to let anyone in.

Even well-liked kids get rejected sometimes. If this happens, and the other kids insist their game is private, your child shouldn't argue. Instead, your child should just calmly walk away and try a different group or maybe approach the same group again, later.

Sometimes kids complain, "The other kids never want to do what I want to do!" It's not a good idea to approach a group that is busy doing one activity and immediately try to persuade them to do a different activity. First, children need to join the ongoing activity of the group. If there's a lull, then they can suggest a new activity.

For older children, joining a group usually involves being part of a conversation. The watch-then-blend strategy that younger kids use to join a game still applies. Your child should listen to the conversation long enough to pick up on the emotional tone. Are the other kids excited? Annoyed? Disgusted? When there's an opening in the conversation, your child should make a comment that has the same emotional tone. For instance, if the other kids are excited about a new movie, your child should pipe in with either an interested question or a similarly enthusiastic comment. If the kids are complaining about the cafeteria food, your child should also complain, perhaps reminiscing about other yucky lunches.

You may want to help your child practice matching the emotional tone of a conversation. You could role-play common conversation topics. For instance, what could your child say if the other kids are

- Complaining about a social studies assignment?

- Excited about how a professional sports team is performing?

- Worried about an upcoming math test?

- Disappointed that a TV show got cancelled?

Matching the emotional tone does *not* mean your child has to lie or robotically follow everyone else. It's about being aware and respectful of others' feelings. For instance, if the kids are complaining about a social studies assignment, your child shouldn't chime in with "I already finished it! It was easy!" That would be a put-down. Your child also doesn't have to pretend to be struggling with it. Saying something like, "Yeah, having to do the bibliography was a pain!" would be honest but also sympathetic.

Encourage Kind Friends

Sometimes kids with low self-esteem stick with a bad friend because they believe they don't have any other options. For instance, they may tolerate a friend who always bosses them around, makes mean comments to them, or ditches them when more desirable friends are around. If you think this is happening with your child, it's important to help your child reflect on what it feels like to be around this person. Every friendship has occasional rough spots, but if your child frequently feels hurt or angry after spending time with a particular friend, it may be time to reevaluate the friendship.

In some cases, it may be possible to maintain a more limited friendship. Your child may be able to enjoy the friend when the friend is being kind and speak up when the friend is being mean. For instance, your child could say calmly, "This isn't fun for me" or "I want a turn." If the friend doesn't respond, your child should walk away. Tolerating meanness will only make it continue.

If the meanness is severe or continuous and speaking up hasn't helped, your child should stop trying to maintain this relationship, because it's not a friendship. Friends care about each other and treat each other with kindness.

The uncertainty of breaking off an unhealthy relationship is scary. No one wants to be alone, so kids tend to cling to the familiar—even if it's painful—rather than risk the unknown. On the other hand, staying in an unhealthy relationship is a guarantee of continued abuse. Your child's time and energy are better invested in cultivating new friendships.

You can help your child by creating opportunities to get together with other kids. This could mean starting a new activity or inviting new friends over. You may want to have your child make a list of kids who might be open to friendship. This could include kids who have chatted with them, worked with them on a project, live nearby, or have similar interests.

Support Gradual Friendship Growth

Sometimes kids with low self-esteem feel bad about themselves because they don't have a close friend. They may have people that they are friendly with, but just not have that special bond with a friend who knows them and supports them. They may look enviously at other kids who all seem to have a best buddy—or two or three—and wonder what is wrong with them that they don't.

Explain that close friendships aren't found; they're built. To have close friends, your child has to invest time and effort into developing relationships.

One of the most important things children can do to deepen a friendship is to get together outside of school. Often kids with low self-esteem are afraid to do this. They think they can't invite people over unless they know them very well. They have it backwards. Inviting someone over is how they start to get to know someone very well. If your kid and another kid have had fun together once, that's a good enough basis to invite that kid over to hang out.

Children with low self-esteem focus on their own discomfort, which gets in the way of their reaching out. They worry, *What if I invite people and they say no?* An invitation is actually a compliment that says *I like you enough to want to spend more time with you*. It's worth taking the chance of inviting someone because there's no harm in asking. Even if the other child says no, the invitation signals an openness to friendship, which makes it easier for the other child to invite your child some other time.

Your child may want to come up with a list of possible people to ask over. That way, if one kid says no, your child can immediately contact the next person on the list. If your child has invited someone three times and they've said no, then probably they are not open to friendship, and your child should move on.

Activity-based get-togethers can ease initial jitters, because kids don't have to worry about what to do. Your child can mention an activity in the initial invitation to the potential friend ("Do you want to see that movie together?" "Would you like to go bowling on Saturday?" "Do you want to come over and bake cupcakes?") or offer a choice of two activities when the potential friend arrives at your home ("Do you want to play air hockey or shoot hoops?" "Do you want to play checkers or make bracelets?")

It's also useful to have different kinds of friends. Not every friend has to be a best friend. Kids might have one friend who makes them laugh, another friend who is good company in band, another friend who is a good partner for school projects, another friend who's a good buddy at summer camp. Over time, some of these friendships may deepen, or they may remain enjoyable, casual friendships. Both close and casual friends are valuable and can give kids that sense of belonging that contributes to real self-esteem.

Wrap-Up

Friendship challenges are common, but kids with low self-esteem are quick to see them as a sign of personal inadequacy. Their self-focus gets in the way of making and keeping friends. Rather than dwelling on flaws, your child needs to avoid off-putting behaviors that push peers away and instead build genuine connections based on common ground with other children. To join in ongoing activities or conversations, your child should first watch and listen, then slide into the action without interrupting.

So far, we've been focusing on the first ingredient of real self-esteem, connection. We've looked at ways to help children build supportive relationships with parents, siblings, and peers. The next two chapters look at the second ingredient of real self-esteem, competence, which refers to gaining skills and embracing learning. Chapter 6 focuses on supporting the child who is quick to give up when things become difficult.

Take-Home Points

- Having even one friend who likes them back helps kids have healthier self-esteem, feel less lonely, have more positive attitudes toward school, be less likely to get bullied, and cope better with stressful events.

- Instead of dwelling on feeling rejected, kids with low self-esteem need to shift to thinking about *What can I offer and to whom?*

- Children can build genuine friendships that support real self-esteem by developing a generous, outward focus rather than an inward, self-critical focus.

- For children, the key to making and keeping friends is not trying to be impressive; it's doing things to make others enjoy spending time with them.

PART 3
COMPETENCE

"I Can't Do It! I Quit!"

When Your Child Gives Up Easily

"I hate soccer! I want to quit!" Lilah announced, throwing her bag down.

"What are you talking about?" her Dad asked. "Last week you said you love soccer!"

"Well, now I don't!" Lilah insisted. "I hate it! I'm no good at it! Today, Coach Jamison said I have to practice my soccer dribbling."

"Okay…"

"No, it's not okay. He hates me!"

"I'm sure he doesn't hate you, Lilah. He's trying to help you improve."

"He said I need to get faster, but I can't do it! He's making us do all these complicated drills, and I'm the worst one on the team!"

"Well, it's your first year playing on the school team… Just stick with it! You'll get better if you keep practicing."

"I'm no good at soccer!" Lilah moaned. "I'm never playing soccer ever again!"

Lilah and her dad are talking past each other. For Lilah, this conversation is about *Am I worthless?* When the coach offers constructive criticism, she immediately feels inadequate. She starts by defensively lashing out: she hates soccer; the coach hates her. Then we see her feelings of hopelessness and inadequacy slip out: she can't do it; she's the worst on the team. These feelings seem so intolerable that she jumps to wanting to quit soccer and avoid the whole mess.

For Lilah's dad, this conversation is about the emotionally neutral topic of *How does one develop soccer skills?* He keeps trying to redirect Lilah toward this more practical view, but Lilah is too tangled up in her self-focus and self-doubt to hear him.

The sermon that Lilah's dad gives is one that pretty much every parent has given: keep trying; you'll improve with practice; effort counts.

Unfortunately, kids like Lilah—who most need this lecture—have trouble absorbing it.

For them, the experience of struggling to do something, or even receiving mild criticism, induces painful self-focus, which they desperately want to escape. They collapse in defeat, overwhelmed by their sense of inadequacy, concluding *I'm just no good.* From that perspective, of course they want to quit!

This chapter will talk about how to help kids with low self-esteem let go of self-doubt enough to be able to embrace effort and persist at challenging tasks.

Grit and Its Relationship to Self-Esteem

Children with low self-esteem often lack what Angela Duckworth calls *grit*, which she defines as "perseverance and passion for long-term goals." Grit is usually measured with a questionnaire. People who are high in grit endorse items such as "I have overcome setbacks to conquer an important challenge" and "I finish whatever I begin" as being very true of them, and they disagree with items such as " I become interested in new pursuits every few months" and "I often set a goal but later choose to pursue a different one" (Duckworth et al. 2007, 1087, 1090). Among adults, higher grit is linked to fewer career changes, going further in formal education, and having a higher GPA in college (Duckworth et al. 2007).

Duckworth and her colleagues have conducted various studies showing a link between grit and better outcomes for teens. For example, high school juniors with higher grit scores are more likely to graduate on time (Eskreis-Winkler et al. 2014). Among contestants in the Scripps National Spelling Bee, grittier teens end up ranking higher than those reporting less grit (Duckworth et al. 2007).

Researchers have questioned the usefulness and predictive power of grit (Credé, Tynan, and Harms 2017). But parents and teachers love the idea of grit! We all want to have kids who are like *The Little Engine That Could*, puffing up the mountain, chanting "I think I can! I think I can!" and then gloriously reaching the top!

Grit tends to be viewed as a personality trait—something people have or don't have to varying degrees. There's often a moralistic tone in discussions of grit, where persistence is seen as virtuous and a lack of persistence seems like a personal failing. As a society, we admire those who persevere through hardship, and we judge negatively those who give up.

This moralistic perspective is not useful, especially when we're talking about kids. Children are constantly changing and growing. Saying or implying "You're weak! You're bad! You're a quitter!" isn't kind, and it isn't motivating for most kids (or adults). A judgmental tone is especially unhelpful when dealing with children with low self-esteem, who are already prone to feeling flawed.

Stories about exceptional stick-to-itiveness aren't inspiring to kids with low self-esteem. They see these cases as either irrelevant or just more evidence of their inadequacy. Shining example stories only resonate if listeners believe that they are like the example. When kids with low self-esteem hear accounts of against-all-odds victories, they think, *If that person could do it, but I can't, I'm even more of a loser than I thought!*

Also, viewing grit as a desirable characteristic assumes that sticking with one thing is the ideal, but that's not necessarily true. There's definitely a place in the world for both generalists and specialists. It's normal to have our interests change and evolve. Sometimes people have to try various activities (or jobs) before finding a good fit. Moreover, no one is gritty all the time. On some days, and in some circumstances, it's easier to persist than on others. It's definitely easier to persist with an activity when we enjoy or care about it than when it seems meaningless or forced. Nevertheless, being able to keep going when the going gets tough is an important skill for children.

What Does Grit Look Like in Children?

For children, grit is often discussed in educational contexts along the lines of "He needs to show grit by practicing his math facts!" This is not what grit is about. Duckworth (2016) emphasizes that it is the personally chosen passion part of grit that allows people to endure struggles. Most of Duckworth's research involves people who are in high school or older. They've already shown at least some sustained commitment to certain activities and are capable of embracing personally meaningful goals that could sustain them for years.

In contrast, the vast majority of children are years, if not decades, away from discovering their long-term interests or genuinely forming long-term goals. They haven't been around long enough or seen enough of the world to be able to do this kind of thinking in a meaningful way. They might say, "I'm going to be an astronaut when I grow up," but we're not going to hold them to this pronouncement.

On the other hand, kids are capable of setting longer-term goals with smaller passions. These could include following all of the instructions to build a giant Lego set (even when it collapses a few times) or shooting a certain number of baskets in a row (even after missing a bunch) or reading all of the books in a series (even though there are a lot of them). Persisting with these types of personally chosen experiences offers important learning opportunities for children and might even constitute child-size grit, which could be a stepping stone toward adult-size grit. But what about when kids have to do something they *don't* like?

Where Kids with Low Self-Esteem Get Stuck

All kids need to learn how to stick with important tasks when the going gets tough. This is a difficult thing for anyone to do. When an activity feels painful, it's extremely tempting to avoid it. We're wired to run from pain. If we just quit a painful task—phew! What a relief! Unfortunately, running away from challenges is a very limiting way to go through life.

For kids with low self-esteem, there's an extra layer of pain on top of struggles because they view their struggles as evidence of their inadequacy. For them, struggles bring on agonizing self-awareness that they are desperate to escape. Being acutely aware of their shortcomings, on top of the pain of the task, makes it extra hard for them to persist.

Here's what *won't* work to help kids with self-esteem develop stick-to-itiveness: lecturing them about the need for perseverance and the importance of strong character. This will only push them further into the trap of self-focus and compound their feelings of inadequacy. Although we intend our pep talk to be inspiring, kids with low self-esteem will hear it as *Here's how you are flawed!*

Instead of focusing on personality, we need to help them direct their attention toward *how to* keep going—not merely that they should persevere! We need to help them view struggles as temporary and see themselves as growing rather than irredeemably inadequate. This allows them to move beyond the paralyzing self-judgment that plagues children with low self-esteem.

Cultivating a Growth Mindset

To be able to persist, children need to believe that their unskilled state is only temporary. They need to be able to see a path from where they are now to where they want to be, and to understand that persistence will help them move forward.

Carol Dweck (2006) and her colleagues have done extensive research on what she calls a *fixed* versus a *growth* mindset. Children with a fixed mindset believe that they are born with a certain amount of ability, and that's it. If they do well, that means they have the ability; if they do poorly, it's a sign they lack that ability and there's nothing they can do to improve. A fixed mindset makes kids very vulnerable to giving up: if they perform poorly or struggle to learn something, they see no reason to keep trying. They believe they've hit a dead end, and they're likely to feel inadequate and focus on their shortcomings.

In contrast, children with a growth mindset believe that they can become better at various skills by continuing to try, getting feedback, and learning new strategies. For them, poor performance is a setback but definitely not the end of the story.

Some researchers have questioned the size, duration, and replicability of certain mindset intervention effects (Li and Bates 2017; Orosz et al. 2017). However, there have been numerous studies linking growth mindset to increased performance and persistence (Haimovitz and Dweck 2017). Moreover, the fact that it's not always easy to convince children that they can become more capable by persevering with difficult tasks doesn't mean we should give up trying to do so!

So, how do we get our kids to embrace a growth mindset? A lecture along the lines of "You should have a growth mindset!" won't help. For kids with low self-esteem, this will just reinforce their tendency to judge themselves harshly. They hear this message as personal criticism (*You should be a better human being!*), and they're already criticizing themselves.

Real Self-Esteem Tips to Try

When children are overly focused on evaluating their performance rather than on gaining competence, it's like they're trying to run while looking over their shoulder. They're looking in the wrong direction, which makes it hard to move forward and increases the likelihood that they'll fall on their faces.

A key to helping children with low self-esteem embrace a growth mindset is to lower the stakes so that effort feels less daunting. When we lower the pain and risk associated with effort, we decrease children's self-focus and avoidance and give them the chance to experience that persistence can pay off.

Continuing to try when things feel hard takes courage. It's a leap of faith to think that continued effort will make things easier and ultimately result in victory. To believe that effort leads to success, children must have many, many such experiences.

In order to persist, kids need

1. To be able to manage emotions, such as frustration and discouragement.

2. To have experienced that sustained effort leads to progress.

3. To embrace goals that are personally meaningful.

Here are some practical ways to help your child do these things.

Help Your Child Manage Frustration and Discouragement

The most pressing issue when your child wants to give up is to address feelings of frustration and discouragement. For kids with low self-esteem, these feelings can be very intense. They trigger painful self-focus, and kids desperately want to escape by quitting or avoiding the task. Learning to tolerate these feelings can help children persist.

Acknowledge Negative Feelings Before Focusing on Coping

We adults tend to want to skip the emotions and go straight to the solution. Unfortunately, when kids are caught up in big feelings, they can't do this. We can't just give kids with low self-esteem a "You can do it!" pep talk when they're feeling discouraged, because they'll just say more emphatically, "I stink at this! I stink at everything!"

Acknowledging their feelings puts us on the same side as our kids. It's a crucial step before they can hear or consider possible solutions. Wrapping children's feelings up in words makes those feelings seem more understandable and therefore more manageable. It's easier for kids to cope with a specific feeling than a general sense that I feel bad! or I'm worthless!

We certainly don't want to agree with their harsh self-judgments, but we can say something along the lines of

- "You're feeling discouraged about _____."

- "You felt embarrassed when _____ happened."

- "You're struggling with _____ right now."

Try to anchor your child's feelings to temporary circumstances by inserting words such as "right now" or "in that situation." This allows you to empathize while reigning in your child's sweeping self-criticism. Adding these qualifiers gently communicates to your child that feelings aren't permanent, which can make them seem more tolerable.

Normalize Struggle and the Ups and Downs of Learning

Children with low self-esteem are afraid of feeling anxious or uncomfortable, because they think distress is a sign that they are flawed or inadequate. They try to avoid activities that bring out these feelings. What they don't understand is that feeling anxious is normal when we're doing something new or challenging. And if we stick with the activity, the anxiety almost always decreases.

One way to explain this to kids is to use the analogy of riding a bike. We can't get to the downhill without doing the uphill. Yes, riding uphill is hard, but the payoff is the thrill of being able to coast down after we reach the top. If your child is able to stick with the struggle part of learning long enough to master a task, that task will become easier and more enjoyable. Can your child think of examples when this has happened? Possibilities include learning a new piece of music, mastering a new skill in a sport, or figuring out how to do a certain type of math problem.

Once your child understands this metaphor, you can use it to encourage persistence when things get tough. You could say something like "You're in the uphill part right now. Stick with it! Pretty soon you'll get to the downhill part, where this feels much easier."

Share Stories of Your Own Struggles

Children look at adults and think that we were always as competent as we are today. Sharing stories of your own struggles might help your child see beyond the current moment of frustration.

If you decide to use this strategy, tread gently with the tone of your stories. If you emphasize the struggle but not the effort, you can unintentionally give your child the message that the difficulty is inborn and unchangeable. For example, if you say "I'm a bad speller, too," your child might conclude that learning this week's spelling list is impossible.

On the flip side, be careful not to imply *I conquered this. What's wrong with you that you can't?* If you present yourself too much in the inspiring example direction, your child is likely to conclude *I'm not good enough.*

To offer hope, present yourself as a fellow traveler. Emphasize that you can relate to the struggle and that you have faith in your child's ability to move past it. For instance, you could say, "I had trouble learning long division, too. It's hard to get the hang of it! Keep practicing! It definitely gets easier."

Downplay Your Child's Comparisons to Others

Children with low self-esteem focus on their own struggles and imagine that everyone else performs effortlessly and flawlessly at all times. This me-versus-them comparison isn't useful, and it intensifies negative self-focus as they tell themselves, *I'm the only one who can't do this!*

Undoubtedly there are kids out there who are better/faster/ smarter than your kid. So what? What other people do is irrelevant. They only thing in your child's control is what he does.

Also, other people's struggles aren't necessarily visible. Above the surface, those kids may look like swans, gracefully gliding along, but underneath the water, they could be paddling furiously!

Offer Effective Praise

It seems intuitively obvious that praising our kids ought to make them feel confident in their abilities, but research tells us that praise can sometimes have unintended consequences (Brummelman, Crocker, and Bushman 2016). In some cases, praise can be effective in helping kids recognize competence and embrace challenges; in other cases, praise can backfire and make children feel less motivated to try challenging tasks. Here's what we do know about effective praise:

Effective praise is sincere and earned. Praise is most meaningful to children when it reflects genuine achievement or improvement. Praising kids for working hard when they know they didn't put in much effort comes across as fake and manipulative. Also, when an adult says, "Good job!" for mediocre performance, children may infer *She thinks this is the best I can do!* This is especially likely if another child isn't praised for the same performance or even gets criticized for it (Meyer 1992). Then the "Good job!" sounds like a consolation prize: *Good job for someone of your limited ability!* That definitely doesn't help kids feel competent. You want your congratulations to mean something, so don't give praise for actions that are trivial. "Good job scratching your elbow!" is not going to help your child feel more competent.

Effective praise isn't overly effusive. It's tempting to gush glowing praise to make up for children with low self-esteem's tendency to put themselves down, but this is likely to backfire (Brummelman, Crocker, and Bushman 2016). Effusive praise feels less believable to children with low self-esteem, because it's so far from their view of themselves. It can place undue pressure on kids, unintentionally conveying the message *You must continue to perform amazingly well!* It can also leave them feeling worthless when they struggle or fail with future tasks. A better bet for kids with low self-esteem is to offer simple positive feedback, acknowledging visible results in a specific area (O'Mara et al. 2006). Comments such as "You did it!" or "You got every problem right! You really understand this concept!" are indisputable. It may be useful to follow up with questions focused on process, such as "What was your strategy?" If your child responds, "I dunno," or insists it was luck, you could offer, "I saw you starting to study on the weekend, so you had plenty of time" or "I noticed that you did all of the problems in the study guide." You could also just say, "Well you may want to think about that, because your strategy definitely paid off."

Effective praise focuses on causes that are controllable. Effort and strategy are within a child's control; innate ability isn't. Praising kids for ability implies that they ought to be able to succeed without trying and that they may as well give up if they struggle. This type of praise is linked to less persistence in children (Henderlong and Lepper 2002). In one study, researchers conducted ten daily interviews with mothers about their responses to their eight- to twelve-year-old children's academic successes, such as doing well on a test or homework assignment (Pomerantz and Kempner 2013). They asked mothers whether they gave *person praise* ("You're so smart!" "You're a good kid!") or *process praise* ("You tried hard!" "You must really enjoy schoolwork!"). The more mothers offered person praise, the more their children believed that intelligence is unchangeable and wanted to avoid challenging tasks at school six months later. Process praise didn't have these negative associations. To give your child process praise, describe what your child did to achieve the success. For example, you could say, "Those seven-times tables are tricky, but you kept practicing them, and now you know them really well!" or "That was a good idea to look at the rubric before you started making your history poster. You figured out exactly what the teacher was looking for and got the project done efficiently."

Effective praise should focus on progress rather than comparison. "You're the best!" praise is risky because that status can change in an instant. It also fosters anxious self-focus (*Am I really the best? What if I stop being the best?*) and feeds into perfectionistic tendencies by implying that children are only worthy if they are number one. Drawing attention to individual progress, on the other hand, can inspire hope. (See "the language of becoming" in chapter 3.) You could say, "Have you noticed how much you've improved on your freestyle time? You've gotten so much faster than you were at the beginning of the swim season. I think all your practice is really paying off!" or "That was lovely. I enjoyed hearing you play that piece! You've really mastered that tricky part in the middle that you struggled with last week."

Show That Strategy Plus Effort Can Lead to Success

Adults frequently lecture children about the importance of effort. But kids with low self-esteem don't see or haven't experienced a connection between effort and success. They hear these lectures as *You should suffer!* For them, continued effort translates to continued proof of their inadequacy, which intensifies their negative self-focus. We need to help them focus on the task rather than on judging themselves, and to create and highlight opportunities for them to experience that continued effort pays off.

Start with Strategy to Minimize Wasted Effort

Just trying hard is no guarantee of success. "I studied for hours, and it didn't help!" is a common complaint from children. When kids try hard but don't get results, they're quick to conclude that all effort is futile. Kids with low self-esteem also make an extra self-focused leap, concluding *Effort is useless, because I can't do anything right!*

Effort without strategy is unproductive and demoralizing. To avoid fruitless effort, help your child figure out a strategy *before* beginning any major project. For instance, does the project have a grading rubric? What does it tell your child about where the teacher thinks the most effort should go? Focusing on strategy at the start of a project is kinder and more effective in making sure your child's efforts bring results than criticizing the project after it's complete. Correcting schoolwork when kids think they're done tends to lead to meltdowns.

If a teacher hasn't set up intermediate steps for a large assignment, you may be able to help your child create them by working backwards. Have your child describe what she wants the end result to be. What's the step immediately before that? And before that? Visualizing the big picture helps kids break down the steps. For example, if your child has to create a video about China, have her imagine what the final product will look like and then think of the necessary steps to make that happen. A video about China might require a map. Will your child draw it or use a picture? It will require a script. What topics will your child cover and who will read the script? It will require some facts. Where will your child find those?

If there's a big test coming up, make sure that your child uses effective study strategies. Kids don't automatically know how to study, so teaching them efficient ways to learn and remember information can save a lot of anguish and wasted effort. Research tells us that the best way to prepare for a test is to practice doing whatever you'll have to do on the test (Dunlosky et al. 2013). For instance, on a math test, your child will have to do math problems. Anything other than doing math problems (paging through notes, watching you do problems, sharpening pencils…) will not prepare your child for the test.

By focusing on strategy, we help kids with low self-esteem let go of unproductive self-criticism and turn their attention and energies toward more productive directions. This makes it more likely that their efforts will lead to success.

Build on Small Successes, So Your Child Sees Progress

It's easier for children to persist when they can see, *Okay, I'm getting somewhere!* Beginning with small, easily achievable goals can help get momentum going.

For instance, if your child feels discouraged because he can't swim the whole length of the pool, you could help him set a goal to swim halfway across. When that feels easy, go for three-quarters of the way. When that feels easy, swimming the whole length won't be so difficult.

Similarly, if your child plays a musical instrument, you could help her learn the strategy of practicing just one measure of a music piece until it's easy before moving onto the next section. Little by little, your child will gain both competence and confidence.

Small successes feel doable and give kids hope. Be careful not to go overboard, helping your child with schoolwork. You can encourage. You can coach. But don't actually touch it. If you take over, your child will know that he doesn't really own the success. Also, for kids with low self-esteem, taking over their work sends the unintended message *You're so hopeless, I have to do it for you!*

Children have to earn their own sense of competence. We can help by making the steps toward competence small enough that they don't seem scary. Your child is also more likely to be able to accept credit for these small successes.

Tell Struggle-Then-Triumph Stories About Your Child

One of the most important ways that we as parents can influence our children is by the stories we tell about them. If we tell stories about our kids quitting, it implies that the next chapter will involve more quitting. On the other hand, telling stories about how they struggled and then triumphed can help inspire them to keep going.

Children with low self-esteem tend to see struggle as a sign that they're incapable of learning or doing a particular task so they should stop. You can put their current difficulties in perspective by recounting times when they managed to persist and it paid off. For example, you could say, "I remember when you were learning to ride your bike. You kept falling and falling, but you also kept trying. And now you're zipping around the neighborhood!"

Stories like these underscore children's past experiences of effort paying off. They make it easier for kids to believe that their current hard work will ultimately lead to success if they don't quit. Tell these stories frequently, not just when your child is feeling discouraged.

Highlight Comparisons Between Your Child's Current and Past Self

Comparing your child's current self with her past self can help her feel less stuck. These comparisons will carry the most impact if they're visual. Pulling out old photos, videos, or adorable old schoolwork might help. Even looking back at an earlier part of a textbook might be useful.

The goal is to help your child see progress and to reinforce the idea that he is learning and growing. Viewing a past self can help children let go of negative self-judgments because it highlights the fact that where they are now is only temporary. It's just one tiny point on a long journey. All they have to do is keep going.

Help Your Child Find Meaningful Goals

Kids have less freedom than adults and often have to do things that adults decide they have to do. But, to the extent that we can, we should support children in pursuing goals that matter to them. This helps them embrace effort and, by enabling them to connect with something bigger than themselves, shifts them away from self-focus.

Choose Activities That Fit Your Child's Strengths

We all have strengths and weaknesses, and it's definitely more pleasant to develop our strengths than to address our weaknesses.

While it's true that most abilities will improve with practice and feedback, it's easier and often more rewarding to focus on areas where we're working with our natural aptitudes.

Unfortunately, kids with low self-esteem often have trouble identifying their strengths. They may even insist that they don't have any. One way to shift this thinking is to have your child complete a free online quiz called the VIA Inventory of Strengths for Youth. This online questionnaire allows children ages ten to seventeen to identify their signature strengths out of a set of twenty-four different possibilities. (For children under ten, you can look at the list of strengths and see which you think best fit your child.) Sample strengths include gratitude, hope, zest, curiosity, fairness, humor, and love (Park and Peterson 2006). Signature strengths aren't about being the world's greatest on some dimension; they're really about the personal qualities that matter most. Helping kids use their signature strengths may lead to a sense of greater competence, well-being, and connection with others (Park and Peterson 2008).

More informally, you can use your own general knowledge of your child to help guide her toward activities that might be a good fit. For instance, if group sports such as soccer and basketball don't appeal to your child, maybe less-common athletic activities—such as fencing, yoga, baton twirling, or diving—would. If your child hates all sports, maybe a drone club, an art or photography class, or a church choir would be a good fit.

What if your child doesn't want to try anything? Find two options that you think might be a good fit and insist that your child choose one for a trial period. Start small. A short introductory class over the summer or a once-a-week class at the local YMCA could give your child enough of a taste to want more.

It may take some trial and error before you find the right activity or activities. The key is to find something that your child will be willing to stick with long enough to see improvement over time. When children do an activity that fits their strengths, they'll find it more enjoyable, so they're more likely to keep doing it. This can lead to further enjoyment, persistence, and growing competence.

Look for a Mentor or Team

Often the best way to encourage kids to persevere at difficult tasks is through their connections to people who matter to them. This type of connection can diffuse painful self-focus that gets in the way of learning.

A mentor can be very inspiring. Mentors are usually *not* a parent or immediate family member. You're too close. An independent but caring voice can get through to your child in a different way. Be creative in seeking out people who might inspire your child. A choir director, a volunteer leader, a favorite aunt, a coach or tutor…any of these people could be the influence that helps your child follow through with effort.

Belonging to a group or team of some sort can also help kids keep going when things are hard, because they don't want to let others down. Teams don't have to be sports related. The key is to help kids feel part of something bigger than themselves.

Find a Rationale That Makes Sense to Your Child

Giving children some choice in what or how they do things makes them more willing to do them. When we can't give them a choice, offering a rationale that makes sense to them may help them buy into a goal and persist in their efforts. Here's the rationale that I've offered to both clients and my own children about why they need to do "stupid" homework. There are two things we learn in school: the what and the how. The *what* has to do with content. What are the four phases of the moon? What are the five causes of the Civil War? People eventually forget a lot of this. But that's okay because the what is just a vehicle for learning the *how*, which has to do with process. How do you get your work done efficiently? How do you figure out what the boss wants? How do you work with other people? You will use the how for the rest of your life.

Don't Pay Your Child for Performance

Sometimes parents are tempted to pay kids for performance. They might give their kids money or toys for every A on their report card or every goal they score in soccer. This is a bad idea. Offering a reward is an external form of motivation that might temporarily inspire a burst of effort, but it doesn't help kids develop the internal motivation that they need to persist long term.

It can also backfire. Many studies show that rewarding kids for doing things that they might do on their own makes them less likely to do those things when the rewards are removed (e.g., Lepper and Henderlong 2000). It's as if the reward convinced kids that *This is only worth doing if I get paid to do it!*

When adults offer rewards for performance, they assume that kids underperform because they don't care enough, but offering rewards doesn't teach children how to do something. When children lack the necessary skills, they won't be able to perform, no matter how enticing the reward. And if they fail to earn the reward, kids with low self-esteem will feel even more dejected.

Competence is its own reward. It feels good to be able to do something well. Far more effective than paying kids to perform is helping them to develop real skills in areas that matter to them.

Know When to Insist on Persistence and When to Let Your Child Quit

Childhood is about exploring, so there's no reason to believe that you'll hit on your child's long-term passion right away. By sampling different activities, children have the opportunity to learn skills and learn about themselves. Parents often struggle with trying to decide if they should make their child continue an activity when the child wants to quit. There are no hard-and-fast rules about this, but here are some questions that might help you decide.

Has your child given it a decent try? For new activities, it's usually best to start with a small commitment: one week, one month, or one season. Some activities take longer than others to master. You may want to strike an agreement ahead of time about what constitutes a decent try. It's also important to help your child learn in the right context. I once took one of my kids to a music teacher who said he believed children should only play scales for the first two years. This shows a profound lack of understanding of children and motivation in general. We didn't go back after that first lesson. My child and I had agreed that he would try lessons for a year, but I found a different, kinder teacher.

Would continuing let your child experience success? If an activity is just not one where your child is going to be successful, then persisting doesn't make sense. When one of my kids took an Irish dance class, we discovered that she has no sense of rhythm and can't keep time with the beat of music. After the first year, when she said she didn't want to continue, I was quick to agree.

How strongly is your child objecting to the activity? If your child is just whining without much emotion, it's probably okay to insist on continuing until the next logical break point. Pay more attention to how your child behaves after doing the activity than to what he says before going. Your child might just be complaining about not wanting to get off the couch. This is common. If your child is cheerful on the way home, that's more indicative of how he actually feels about the activity.

Would other people be negatively affected by your child quitting? In addition to your child's feelings about the activity, an important consideration is how other people might be affected if your child were to quit an activity. Sometimes, for the greater good, children just have to tolerate difficult situations with a cooperative attitude. Other times, it's better for everyone's sake to move on.

Wrap-Up

Children with low self-esteem tend to quit easily because they see their struggles as a sign of inadequacy. They get trapped by their negative self-focus, telling themselves, *I'm no good. I can't do this. There's no hope.*

Helping your child learn to persist won't be easy or quick. Sermons about the virtues of stick-to-itiveness are likely to make your child feel even more flawed. Instead, emphasize that frustration and discouragement are normal and temporary. Look for opportunities to help your child learn that effort plus effective strategy will pay off. It will be easiest for your child to persist with activities that your child finds meaningful.

The next chapter will look at one of the most painful heartbreaking problems of children with low self-esteem: their tendency to be harshly self-critical.

Take-Home Points

- Kids need child-size goals to develop child-size grit.

- Teach children with low self-esteem *how to* keep going by focusing on effective learning strategies, rather than just telling them that they *should* persevere.

- The connection between effort and outcome is learned. If your child hasn't experienced that effort pays off, it's hard to keep trying.

- Connecting with a mentor, team, or area of learning that they want to master helps kids with low self-esteem move beyond paralyzing self-focus to embrace effort.

"It's Not Good Enough!"

When Your Child Suffers with Harsh Self-Criticism and Perfectionism

"Oh, no! I ruined it! I dripped paint and now my whole painting is wrecked!" James moaned.

"Let me see, James," Mrs. Steiner, the art teacher, said. "Oh, it's fine. The drip is hardly noticeable. You can leave it or just paint over it."

"No, it's all messed up!" James insisted. "It's supposed to be a bird, and if I paint over it, the body will be too pointed."

"How about turning that into a branch?"

"No, that would look horrible!"

"You could also cut out the bird and put it on a new piece of paper, like a collage."

"No! My whole painting is terrible!" James wailed, becoming more and more upset. "I'm going to rip it up!"

"Really, James, you've put a lot of effort into this painting. I think it's good. It doesn't have to be perfect. And anyway, you did a great job with the sky, and I really like how you did the leaves and grass," Mrs. Steiner said reassuringly.

"Why did I drip that paint?" James asked tearfully. "It's completely ruined! I'm so stupid! I can't do anything right!"

●

James made a mistake on his painting. Despite his teacher's efforts to offer reassurance and constructive suggestions, James insists that the painting is completely ruined. In fact, the teacher's comments seem to make James more upset rather than less. He ignores all of the teacher's positive remarks and jumps quickly from saying the painting is ruined to concluding that he is utterly incompetent.

One of the ironies of self-esteem is that it has very little to do with objective performance. Children (and adults) who are outwardly very capable and accomplished may be cruelly self-critical and plagued by feelings of inadequacy. They may drive themselves brutally hard, trying to live up to unachievable standards, then collapse in dejection when they fall short. They may relentlessly pursue achievement as a way of bolstering their self-worth while feeling that their accomplishments are never really satisfying. Failures are excruciatingly humiliating, and victories offer only fleeting relief in the face of their intense feelings of worthlessness. Every achievement just ramps up what they believe they have to do in future performances. Nothing they do ever feels good enough. In contrast to children with low self-esteem who avoid effort (focused on in chapter 6), these children with low self-esteem push themselves mercilessly, flogging themselves with self-criticism. Harsh self-criticism is not only painful but also a risk factor for depression, especially when coupled with stressful events (Kopala-Sibley et al. 2015).

Causes of Harsh Self-Criticism

But where does this harsh self-criticism come from? Certainly some children learn it by internalizing the reactions of extremely critical, demanding, and abusive parents who give them the message that approval is contingent upon achievement or that they are unworthy of love (Blatt 1974, 2004). However, in my practice, most parents of children with low self-esteem are alarmed and dismayed by the vicious way their kids criticize themselves. They argue vigorously when they hear their children put themselves down, which only seems to intensify their children's self-criticism.

It's possible that some self-critical children are overly sensitive to typical parental reprimands and distort these into harsh self-judgments. Other children may develop excessive self-criticism or even self-hatred through being rejected by peers (Kopala-Sibley et al. 2013). Poorer performance than peers or failure in academic or other areas could lead to chronic self-criticism, but the opposite is also true. Kids who routinely do very well can become terrified of not being able to live up to their reputations (Damian et al. 2017). Stressful events may also trigger self-criticism. For instance, children whose parents get divorced often blame themselves for the breakup, in part because it's easier to believe they are "bad" than to accept that they have no control over negative events.

Tempering Self-Criticism

Self-criticism, when it becomes a habit, can be devilishly hard to change. Children can become very attached to their self-criticism, believing that it is somehow virtuous or even necessary to attack themselves. They may think that they "deserve" to beat themselves up, because they are so flawed, and they use self-criticism as a form of self-punishment. They may also jump to self-criticism to get in front of the criticism that they imagine is forthcoming from others: if they rip themselves to shreds first, no one else will have a chance to do so! Or they may believe that treating themselves cruelly is the only way to spur themselves on toward achievement. They assume that without this harshness, they would be lazy and do nothing.

Of course, we want our children to strive for excellence, but harsh self-criticism hurts rather than helps performance. When kids embrace healthy striving, they feel inspired and energized. Harsh self-criticism, on the other hand, feels desperate, forced, and relentless.

Breaking through the habit of self-criticism requires gentleness and persistence from parents. This chapter will discuss ways to help children avoid self-attacks, handle competitions and tests, and learn more compassionate ways to treat themselves.

Real Self-Esteem Tips to Try

To help children with low self-esteem let go of vicious self-criticism, we definitely need to address their negative comments, but, more importantly, we need to help them change the thinking behind these comments and teach them other ways of responding in situations that tend to trigger self-criticism. Here are some strategies that can help you guide your child toward breaking this painful habit.

Defusing and Avoiding Self-Attacks

The most urgent issue for parents of self-critical kids is how to respond to their self-attacks. If we follow our instincts, arguing and protesting their harsh comments, we may accidentally encourage even more vicious self-criticism. Knowing that these comments get a big reaction from us makes kids see them as powerful. They may even view self-criticism as a useful way to get reassurance. But our reassurances don't sink in. The more we say, "You're a great kid!" the harder children with low self-esteem argue, "I'm the worst kid in the world!"

Self-critical children dive into the task of ripping themselves apart with gusto! Because they are so immersed in looking at their (perceived) flaws, they fail to see the broader picture. Stepping back from this intense negative self-focus can help them put their mistakes in perspective.

Address Mean Comments

If arguing will backfire, what should we say when our kids put themselves down? Start by acknowledging the feelings behind the self-criticism. For instance, you could say

"You're feeling frustrated about…"

"You're disappointed that…"

"You're worried that…"

"You're discouraged because…"

"You wish…"

When you focus on feelings rather than evaluations, you place yourself *with* rather than against your hurting child and provide understanding that eases your child's burden. You also help your child make sense of the experience and make it clear that negative feelings don't have to lead to hopeless negative judgments of the entire self, for all time, in all situations.

You may also want to offer a gentle hug. A hug offers comfort and acceptance, and these are the exact opposite of self-directed mean comments.

But what if you've spent time acknowledging your child's feelings in multiple ways, and your child just makes nastier and nastier self-critical comments? At some point, you may need to draw the line by saying "It's not okay to say mean things about someone I love." This makes it clear that you don't like these comments, without getting into a debate about them. What if your child wants to argue even about your love, saying something like "You shouldn't love me, because I do everything wrong!" Just repeat, "It's not okay to say mean things about someone I love."

A word of warning: If you make this comment, be prepared to have it thrown back at you. A mom I worked with once said aloud, "Oh, I'm so stupid!" after she made a minor mistake. Her daughter promptly insisted, "It's not okay to say mean things about someone I love!" The mom smiled and said, "You're absolutely right!"

Embrace Realistic Standards

Children with low self-esteem imagine only two categories when they evaluate their work: perfect and worthless. If their work isn't perfect, then it must be worthless. This is a trap because perfection is extremely rare.

Voltaire once said, "The perfect is the enemy of the good." Can your child explain what this means? Perfectionistic standards can get in the way of children starting or finishing work, and they definitely interfere with the playfulness and risk-taking necessary for creativity.

If your child seems anxious about starting or finishing a project, it may be worth having a conversation about what a "barely adequate" or "just okay" job might look like. If it's a school project with a grading rubric, that can help identify minimum requirements. Encourage your child to get the "just okay" job done first. Maybe your child won't be satisfied with that. If there's time, your child can do more; if not, at least the basics have been covered. Either way, it's healthier to try to meet and maybe exceed a standard of "just okay" than to be distraught over the idea of falling short of an unattainable or too costly standard of absolute perfection.

Children with low self-esteem often imagine that demands are much larger and more complicated than they really are. I worked with a young girl who was terrified when the teacher said the class would be doing daily journal writing. She tearfully told me that she didn't know what to write. She didn't have any good ideas! She'd never be able to come up with anything! This girl imagined that she'd have to write pages upon pages of clever prose. She was a voracious reader, and I think she thought she would have to create a journal like some of the best-selling diary books she enjoyed reading. It turned out that the teacher only wanted a few sentences. The writing period was just fifteen minutes. I suggested she describe what "special" class she had each day ("Today is Tuesday. We have chorus...") or what she had for lunch, and the task seemed much more doable.

The teacher can be a good ally in helping your child embrace realistic standards and avoid overdoing. Your child might be surprised to hear how little time the teacher expects kids to spend on an assignment. If you contact the teacher ahead of time to explain what's happening, the teacher could set some sanity-preserving limits for your child, such as "Don't write more than one page" or "Don't spend more than half an hour working on this." The teacher could also schedule progress check-ins to make sure your child is on-track with larger projects or give your child permission to stop at a certain point.

Put Mistakes in Context

If your child is upset about a less-than-perfect project or performance that has already happened, acknowledge the disappointment ("You wish you'd played that one part correctly"), but also encourage your child to think about what went right.

If your child says, "Nothing! It was completely terrible!" you might have to explain that there are many aspects to a good performance and use some questions to broaden your child's narrow focus on mistakes. Seeing the big picture causes mistakes to shrink to their proper size.

For instance, in the case of a musical performance, you might ask how many notes your child got right. Was your child able to keep the rhythm or coordinate with other performers? Did your child use crescendos and phrasing to convey the musical feel of the piece? Did your child make it all the way through to the end? Did your child have the courage to get on stage and perform? That alone is a victory! I tell clients, "Parents think you look cute just sitting (or standing) there. Anything you do beyond that is just icing on top!"

You may also want to ask your child how many members of the audience came to the performance expecting to see perfection. The answer, of course, is none. If they'd wanted a perfect performance, they could have stayed home and listened to the piece played by a computer, with perfect pitch and perfect timing. The audience wanted to see something much more exciting than perfection: ongoing learning and growth, effort, and love of music (or other perfomance art).

In my practice, I often encourage perfectionistic kids to experiment with making some small mistakes *on purpose*. This can be a powerful way to break the stranglehold of misery-inducing worries about having to do things perfectly. Usually, no one notices the errors, but even if someone does, it's no big deal. The feared consequences ("Someone will laugh at me!" "They'll think I'm stupid!" "She'll be mad!") either don't happen or they're survivable.

Take a Mental Step Back

When children are trapped in a self-critical rut, they tend to be very emotional. They may cry or yell. Their bodies look tense and agitated as they focus narrowly and relentlessly on their failings. They definitely aren't able to think in useful ways about their situation or how to move forward.

There's growing evidence from Ethan Kross and his colleagues (2017, 2011b) that *self-distancing*, which means getting an observer's perspective on a situation, may be useful for helping children lower the intensity of their emotional reactions and think more clearly.

So how do we help kids step back? With very young children and children who are acutely upset, I recommend being concrete about it. Have them close their eyes, breathe in, exhale deeply, and then open their eyes and physically move away from the situation by taking several steps back or moving into another room.

Kross and his colleagues' research points to some other possible self-distancing strategies children can use:

1. Imagine the scene from far away. What would a fly on the wall see? What would someone watching from the ceiling see?

121

2. Talk about the situation as if they were a narrator or news commentator, referring to themselves by name rather than saying "I." For instance, in the scene at the beginning of this chapter, James could tell himself, "James dripped some paint. What could James do next?"

3. Pretend to be someone else approaching the situation. For example, in one study, researchers found that four- to six-year-olds who pretended to be Batman or Dora the Explorer persisted longer on a repetitive task (White et al. 2017). Older kids might prefer pretending to be a confident peer.

Match the Effort to the Importance

Not all projects deserve the same level of effort. Often, getting something done is more important than getting it perfect.

You may want to discuss with your child the idea of *reasonable effort*. For instance, if your child has to write a paragraph, he could spend hours writing and rewriting each O to make sure it's perfectly round. Would that be reasonable effort? Of course not! That's silly. Your child has much more interesting things to do than measuring Os. It's worth accepting imperfect Os to make time for other activities.

Reasonable effort depends on the importance of the task, how much time is available, what other competing activities exist, and even how your child is feeling. It's not always possible or necessary for kids to give their best effort.

It may help to ask, "How much time is this project worth?" Some projects deserve only a quick dash to get them done. Some deserve more sustained effort. But here's something I believe deeply: no project is worth kids driving themselves to the point of misery, isolation, and exhaustion. In our crazy age of performance pressure, this is a difficult but vital message to get across to our children.

If your child is sobbing and exhausted, step in and say, "That's enough. Whatever you've done is enough." Your child *won't* thank you for this. You'll get desperate protests about "It's terrible!" or "I'll flunk!" or "My teacher will be mad!" Stand your ground. You may have to confiscate papers, books, or electronics. Tell your child, "You are more important to me than any grade" and "No one expects or wants you to make yourself miserable and exhausted."

Don't do the work for your child, because that buys into the idea that perfect performance is necessary. In the morning, your child can talk with the teacher and figure out how to move forward in a less pressure-filled way. You can offer support and coaching, but your child will feel more empowered if she can address the issue directly than if you speak for her.

But what if the teacher isn't sympathetic or helpful? Worst case, your child will get a bad grade on this project and learn that the world doesn't end if that happens.

Teach Your Child to Accept Compliments

The flip side of avoiding harsh self-criticism is being able to accept genuine compliments. Children with low self-esteem often have a hard time doing this. In fact, when someone says something positive about them, they squirm uncomfortably and immediately launch into a list of reasons why they don't deserve the compliment: "Oh, no, it wasn't good! I messed up this part! I should have done that better! He did it better! She does it more!" They are focused on their own discomfort and self-criticism, but the message they're giving to the person complimenting them is *You don't know anything! Your judgment and taste are terrible! Your kind comment is ignorant and just plain wrong!*

Explain to your child the message that rejecting a compliment sends. Surely your child doesn't mean to insult someone who is being kind!

Then teach your child the appropriate response to a compliment. Smile and say thank you. No excuses. No contradictions. Just a simple thank you. Have your child practice this.

Handling Competition and Tests

Situations that involve outside evaluations are terrifying for self-critical children. Although they're not shy about putting themselves down, competitions, auditions, and tests seem unbearably frightening because they're convinced that their worst self-criticisms will be publicly confirmed.

These children need help lowering the stakes, so they can try without feeling like their entire worth as a human being is up for judgment during every evaluation experience. Children with low self-esteem need to understand that setbacks and mistakes are temporary and a normal part of learning.

Let Your Child Lose

Winning feels good, but it's unrealistic for any of us to believe that we will win every contest. If your child is extremely scared of competing, you may need to help him gradually build up his tolerance for losing.

Start with simple *beat your own record* contests. How far can your child jump? How many times can your child hit a balloon in the air without letting it drop? How long can your child balance on one foot with eyes closed? Attempting these activities several times will yield different results—sometimes winning and sometimes losing. Your child will quickly see that performance varies, and it's easy enough to try again.

From there, you can try cooperative games where all players work together and win or lose as a group. (https://familypastimes .com has some excellent cooperative games.) Then you can try very quick competitive card games such as Blink or Spot It which are over in a few minutes.

Kids-against-the-grown-ups games are a particularly fun way to learn to handle competition. If the adults win, well, that's not surprising. But if the kids win, that's thrilling!

Eventually, your child may want to try organized sports. Sports teams have rituals at the end of games, such as giving high fives to everyone on the opposing team, to emphasize the importance of good sportsmanship.

The point of all of these activities is to help your child recognize that winning and losing are temporary states. You can also emphasize this by asking your child "How long do you think winning or losing lasts?" Say, for example, your child is in a tennis match. After the match, teammates, coaches, and family members will say, "Good game!" "Nice try!" or "Congratulations!" Then everyone moves on to the next thing. Total duration of victory or defeat: five minutes or less.

Yes, it's disappointing to lose, but your child can definitely learn to be strong enough to handle temporary disappointment. With practice, she may even come to enjoy the fun and excitement of a challenging game, regardless of the outcome.

Challenge "Second Best Is the Same As Failure" Thinking

Self-critical children spend a lot of time thinking about how they stack up against others, because they're convinced that being anything less than the best is the same as failing. If your child is a sports fan, here's a way to break through that rigid thinking. Ask your child to identify the very best player in a favorite sport. Then ask, "Does that mean the other players, who aren't as good, should give up and go home? Why not?" Depending on the sport, the answer to why these less-than-number-one athletes should continue might be

- Because the number one athlete couldn't win without them.

- Because they are still excellent athletes, even though they aren't number one.

- Because they have important skills that contribute to the team.

- Because they keep improving as they practice and gain more experience.

- Because they love playing the game, even though they aren't number one.

You could have a similar discussion identifying the best artist, singer, musician, composer, author… There's always room—and need—for more than a single shining star.

Manage Fears of Failing

Sometimes self-critical children walk out of a test convinced that they failed but later learn that they actually did well. While other kids might deliberately attempt to lower expectations by saying they did poorly, children with low self-esteem truly believe they bombed. Their fear of failing distorts their impression of how they did. The fact that they've done well on previous tests doesn't matter. This time they're sure they failed, and there's no convincing them otherwise! Don't try. Acknowledge the feelings without getting sucked into a debate by saying "You're worried that you might not have done as well as you wanted. We'll deal with that when and if it happens."

Sometimes children's negative self-focus can even bring about the failure they fear by causing them to choke on a test. Their mind empties of everything they knew as they dwell painfully and unproductively on how inadequate they are. Becoming more aware of *how* they are thinking (not just the content of their thoughts) can help children learn to avoid this.

Tell your child to imagine two students who don't know the answer to a test question. One student follows up that initial *I don't know!* with *task-relevant thoughts*. This student might evaluate possible answers (*Well, it can't be B. That doesn't make sense!*) or pull up related memories (*Okay, I remember the teacher said something about…*).

The other student follows up that initial *I don't know!* with *task-irrelevant thoughts* along the lines of *Oh, no! I'm going to flunk! I'm so stupid! My parents are going to kill me! I'll never get into a good college! My whole life is ruined!* None of these thoughts are useful for coming up with an answer to the test question.

Everyone's mind wanders sometimes, even in a test situation. The key is not to get stuck in a destructive spiral of harsh self-criticism. Trying *not* to think task-irrelevant thoughts is likely to intensify them in the same way that trying *not* to think about a white bear makes polar bears leap to mind. Encourage your child just to notice task-irrelevant thoughts, without trying to suppress them, and then to gently bring attention back where it belongs. Sometimes using an image can help kids set aside a task-irrelevant thought. This could involve picturing a big, red "irrelevant" stamped on the thought or imagining placing the thought on a high shelf, out of the way, or sweeping the thought off the desk with a small whisk broom and then softly turning back to the task at hand.

Encourage Mastery Goals

A classic distinction in psychology is between mastery and performance goals. *Mastery goals* involve trying to gain competence and improve skills. *Performance goals* involve trying to demonstrate ability, outperform others, or avoid seeming incompetent. Put another way, mastery goals are about learning whereas performance goals are about looking good. Children with low self-esteem tend to focus on performance goals, which intensifies their negative self-focus, interferes with learning, and adds to their misery (Linnenbrink et al. 1999).

Performances and assessments of various sorts are part of life. The trick is to help our children see them not as a measure of their worth but as a sign of where they are just at this point in time. Here's one way to explain this concept:

On a piece of paper, draw a horizontal line with an arrow at the end pointing to the right. Tell your child, "This is a picture of your progress learning math." (You can choose any topic, but we'll use math for this example.) Mark the line a little way in from the left side. Say, "When you were very little, you learned to count. How are you feeling about that counting thing? Are you pretty confident that you know how to count? Excellent! You've mastered counting. Then you learned to add two numbers…" Continue making marks on the line, moving from left to right, to indicate increasingly complex math skills. Be sure to mention lots of examples of things your child has already mastered. Explain that each quiz or test is not a measure of your child's smartness but instead a measure of the extent to which your child has mastered a specific skill *at this particular moment*. No quiz or test or performance is the final word on your child's ability, because it's always possible to keep learning and understand more.

Prevent Self-Handicapping

When the stakes feel too high—which happens often for children with low self-esteem—kids may resort to self-handicapping. This involves creating a ready-made excuse for failure before attempting a task. For instance, a child who is afraid of failing a test might avoid studying, then do frantic cramming at the last minute. That way, when the bad grade comes, the child can think, *I didn't have enough time!* or *I could have done better if I'd tried!*

Self-handicapping is obviously not a healthy strategy, but it's rarely conscious. If your child tends to procrastinate, you may need to step in to help plan a productive and more humane schedule for getting things done. Breaking a task into small steps may make it seem less overwhelming.

Encouraging Self-Compassion

In addition to avoiding harsh self-attacks and learning to tolerate performance situations, self-critical children need to learn to be kind to themselves. Research with adults and teens has shown that teaching self-compassion can ease depression, anxiety, and self-criticism (Germer and Neff 2013; Shahar 2013).

Kristin Neff (2003) highlights three key themes in self-compassion:

1. *Self-kindness rather than self-judgment*, which means being able to respond in gentle and caring ways to our failures, struggles, and flaws.

2. *Common humanity rather than isolation*, which means recognizing that we are all imperfect, and we all struggle, so suffering is part of life for everyone.

3. *Mindfulness rather than overidentification*, which means noticing our painful thoughts and feelings without getting stuck dwelling on them.

Many children with low self-esteem are reluctant to be kind to themselves, because they believe it's necessary or even morally desirable to treat themselves badly. It takes lots of practice to help them learn to feel comfortable treating themselves with kindness. Here are some ways to encourage self-compassion in your child.

Model Kind Self-Talk About Mistakes

Kids learn more from what we do than from what we say. We can lecture them until we're blue about the importance of self-compassion, but unless they see us treating ourselves gently, they won't believe that this is something they can and should do. Use ordinary minor mistakes to model kind self-talk. When you spill the milk or lose your keys, forget an appointment, or drive in the wrong direction, let your child hear you make comments like these:

"Everyone makes mistakes."

"I'll just try again."

"I guess I need to ask for help."

"Oh, well, I can fix it."

"Next time, I'll try a different strategy."

"It's not perfect, but it's done."

"Oops! I messed up part of it, but it's good enough."

Ask, "What Would You Say to a Friend?"

In most cases, children with low self-esteem would never dream of saying to anyone else the mean things they routinely say to themselves. A classic self-compassion question is "What would you say to a friend?" This question can help children shift toward a gentler way of responding to their own mistakes and struggles. Possible answers include

"It's a hard thing you're dealing with right now."

"You'll get through it."

"Stay strong. It'll be okay."

"Just keep trying. You can do it."

"This would be hard for anyone. Keep going."

Note that these comments don't deny your child's suffering but instead acknowledge it warmly and encourage persistence. You may want to help your child come up with a bunch of gentle, encouraging statements to write on index cards for reading over when he needs a little self-compassion.

It may be useful for your child to name the *self-compassionate voice*. This voice counters the self-critical voice not through aggressive arguing but through warmth and understanding. Younger kids may be willing to draw a picture of their internal comforter.

Encourage Using Gentle Touch to Self-Soothe

Neff (2011) suggests gentle touch as a way to comfort ourselves. For kids, this is a beautiful way to make self-compassion concrete. During a calm moment, have your child try different types of soothing touch to see which ones feel most appealing. Do this together, so your child doesn't feel embarrassed. For instance, you each could try gently hugging your own arms, softly stroking your own face, or (my favorite) placing one or two hands on your heart and just noticing the weight and heat between the open palms and the chest. Once your child has identified a pleasant type of gentle touch, she can try using it to quiet self-criticism.

Schedule Enjoyable Activities

Self-critical children sometimes get into a pattern where they believe they have to work all the time. They tell themselves they can't afford to take any time off, or they don't deserve a break, because they haven't worked well enough or accomplished enough.

Everyone needs breaks. These aren't a waste of time; they're a means of refueling.

This is another strategy that we have to teach by doing. Let your child see you deliberately taking time to do fun things on your own, with friends, or with your family. Also help your child plan fun activities. Some children with low self-esteem have trouble figuring out what they'd enjoy doing or are reluctant to let themselves have time off. Do it anyway. Yes, work has to be done, but life isn't meant to be constant drudgery.

Emphasize That Love Doesn't Have to be Earned

Perhaps the most important intervention for self-critical children is to help them understand that being perfect isn't a requirement for being loved. Ask your child, "Would you love me more if I were five pounds lighter? How about if I earned $5,000 more per year?" Of course not! You could do a similar exercise asking about your child's friends. I once asked a very self-critical client whether her best friend was the smartest girl in the whole school. She said no. Was she the most attractive girl in the school? No. Was she the kindest girl? Still no. I said, "Well, if she's not the smartest, prettiest, or kindest, maybe you should dump her!" My client laughed, and I pointed out that, just as she didn't expect her friend to be perfect, her friend probably didn't expect her to be perfect, either.

Wrap-Up

Harsh self-criticism is one of the most painful and persistent characteristics of children with low self-esteem. You may find it upsetting to hear such mean self-judgments, but your child will be reluctant to change this habit, seeing it as necessary, morally righteous, and deserved. Avoid arguing about your child's self-criticism, because that will only make your child more insistent. Helping your child focus on learning rather than performing can ease pressure and contribute to your child becoming more competent. Ultimately, the goal is to help your child realize that love doesn't have to be earned.

The next couple of chapters will focus on the third C of real self-esteem: choice. This involves helping children find their voice, figure out what matters to them, and connect with something bigger than themselves. Chapter 8 talks about the struggles that children with low self-esteem face with feeling indecisive and helpless.

Take-Home Points

- Harsh self-criticism is not only painful but also a risk factor for depression.

- Children with low self-esteem need to embrace learning and experience the fact that setbacks and mistakes are normal and temporary.

- Practicing self-compassion can help children learn to feel comfortable with being kind to themselves.

PART 4
CHOICE

"I Can't Decide!"

When Your Child Feels Trapped by Indecision and Helplessness

"Oh, these are so pretty!" Stacey's grandmother said, admiring the store display of brightly colored bracelets. "Do you like them?"

"Yeah!" Stacey replied enthusiastically. "Lots of girls at my school have them. They're really popular."

"Well, how about if I get you one as a birthday present? Which do you like best?"

"I don't know," Stacey said.

"The blue one is nice..." her grandmother offered.

"Yes, but purple is my favorite color!"

"Okay, let's get the purple one!"

"But, I really like the blue one, too, and the red one would match my sweater..."

"Uh-huh. So, which one do you want?" her grandmother asked.

"I don't know!" Stacey moaned. "This is so hard! What if I choose wrong? I'm bad at choosing! You pick, Grandma!"

"But it's your present, Stacey! I want you to have the one you like best."

"I can't! I can't decide! I don't know which one to get. I never know what to pick! I always pick the wrong thing!" Stacey said, blinking back tears.

●

Stacey and her grandmother are having a good time until Stacey has to make a decision. It's a small decision, but Stacey finds it overwhelming. What should be a pleasant treat becomes a trigger for painful self-focus as she berates herself. Her comments jump quickly from the merits of different bracelets to her personal inadequacy. "I'm bad at choosing!" she insists. Stacey is terrified of making the wrong choice and quickly collapses into helpless paralysis.

Stacey's upset isn't about the bracelets; it's about her uncertainty, which she finds unbearable and interprets as a personal flaw. She's afraid to choose, because she doesn't want to make a choice that she'll later regret. She also feels stupid because she can't decide what she wants. For kids like Stacey, negative feelings such as uncertainty, worry, or discouragement spiral quickly to negative thoughts about the self.

Reactions like Stacey's are exasperating for adults. What's the big deal? It's just a bracelet! Picking the wrong bracelet is very unlikely to be a life-altering decision, so getting all worked up about it seems ridiculous. It's tempting to demand, "Just pick one!" but increasing the pressure to decide is likely to trigger a full-blown meltdown.

So what should we do when our kids get all tangled up about making a decision? In the story above, Grandma needs to acknowledge Stacey's feelings. The trigger for her upset may seem trivial, but her distress is real. Grandma could respond, "You're having trouble deciding which one you want" or "You're feeling overwhelmed by this choice" or "You're worried that you'll choose one and change your mind later." After that, her best bet is probably to distract Stacey and come back to the decision later when Stacey is feeling calmer. It's hard for anyone to think clearly when emotions are running high. Longer term, Stacey definitely needs to learn strategies for making decisions and tolerating uncertainty.

Getting Stuck in Rumination

Children with low self-esteem often struggle with making decisions and taking action. They easily get caught up in a kind of miserable, endless fretting known as *rumination*. This involves repetitive, unproductive thinking about negative feelings and problems and their implications for the self. It's a kind of mental wheel spinning, focused on the symptoms, causes, meanings, and consequences of distress. Everyone ponders big decisions and distressing events, but unhealthy rumination involves getting stuck in negative thinking. Brooding like this may feel productive—because it can take a lot of effort and time to fret—but it isn't. It intensifies misery and low self-esteem and gets in the way of coping (Nolen-Hoeksema, Wisco, and Lyubomirsky 2008).

Exciting new research shows that teaching teens to reduce their habit of rumination can lower their risk for depression and anxiety (Topper et al. 2017). Although teens can certainly reflect on their thinking and emotional experiences in more sophisticated ways than younger kids can, we know that children as young as five or six are capable of talking about how they manage negative feelings, and they understand that deliberately changing how they think can help them feel better (Davis et al. 2010). I strongly believe that the elementary school years are an excellent time in which to begin to teach children about rumination and what to do instead. This could set the stage for a lifetime of better mental health.

This chapter will look at ways to help children recognize and minimize rumination, make decisions, and use more active coping strategies.

Real Self-Esteem Tips to Try

Cultivating real self-esteem in children like Stacey means helping them find their voice and their strength by quieting their unrelenting self-doubt. Children with low self-esteem too often get mired in helplessness. They talk themselves into self-fulfilling prophecies: "There's nothing I can do. It won't work. There's no point in trying. See? It turned out badly, like I knew it would!" To change this tendency, we need to address how they think and help them gain experience acting decisively and effectively.

Breaking Through Rumination

Rumination can be a habit triggered by negative feelings, negative events, or even the possibility of negative events. To break out of this painful and unproductive response, children need to recognize when they're doing it and do something else instead.

Recognize Rumination

Explain to your child that rumination involves going over and over upsetting thoughts without getting anywhere. A metaphor can be a useful way to help kids understand what rumination feels like. Possibilities include a hamster on a wheel, a person running on a treadmill, an iPod stuck on replay, or a car spinning its wheels on ice. What you want to convey is the waste of energy and lack of progress involved in rumination. Rumination is about being mentally stuck. The more we ruminate, the more helpless we feel.

Next, help your child come up with some quick strategies to break free of the trap of rumination. Brief distractions with enjoyable activities can be useful. Exercise is a good distraction. So is taking a shower or listening to music. Reading or drawing or squeezing putty can also work. See what appeals to your child.

Isn't distraction just avoiding problems? Not if it's brief and not if your child's continued pondering is only leading to greater upset. Distraction can help your child get out of the rut of rumination. After that, he can shift to more productive ways of thinking things through and responding.

Learn to Ask Useful Questions

Rumination typically focuses on vague and judgmental *why* questions (Topper et al. 2014). You may have heard your child say things like "Why am I so stupid?" "Why does this keep happening to me?" "Why can't things be easier for me?" or "Why can I never do anything right?" Nothing useful will come from dwelling on these questions! And they're guaranteed to make your child feel more upset.

More targeted questions can suggest a path forward and lead to productive problem solving rather than endless rumination (Watkins 2016). I recommend considering questions that begin with "What can I…?" It takes practice to learn to do this kind of productive thinking instead of ruminating. You may want to work with your child to come up with some useful questions to write on index cards, so she can consult them when needed. Here are some possibilities:

- *What can I do to solve this?*

- *What can I do to make things a little bit better?*

- *What can I try that might help?*

- *What can I do as a first step to get started?*

- *What can I do next?*

- *What can I do to make it more likely things will go well?*

- *What can I do to prevent this from happening again?*

- *What can I do differently next time?*

- *What can I do while I'm waiting to find out?*

- *What can I do to get more information?*

- *What can I do to help me decide?*

- *What can I learn from this?*

Visit http://www.newharbinger.com/40491 to download this list of questions.

Save It for Later

Children often get stuck ruminating at bedtime. Maybe it's because they're lying quietly alone, but suddenly all of their worries, concerns, and regrets leap out, and they insist on talking about them *right now*.

This is not a good idea. Everything seems more overwhelming when we're tired. Also, your child may be tempted to come up with more and more worries, so he can continue talking and delay bedtime. Chatting with your child before bedtime can be a cozy routine, but keep the topics positive.

If your child's mind becomes flooded with worries after being tucked into bed, have your child write them down on small pieces of paper and put them in an empty tissue box. There's no need for full sentences or correct spelling. Just a few words or even a small picture will do. Then at a scheduled time the next day (nowhere near bedtime), the two of you can spend no more than fifteen minutes discussing the topics in the box. If you don't finish, you can continue the conversation at the same scheduled time the following day.

Having a scheduled time for discussing worries can be a stepping stone for your child toward worrying less. When your child gets to the point of not having enough worries to fill the fifteen minutes, use that time to do something fun together.

What if your child says she can't sleep because of "bad thoughts"? What I often tell children in my practice is that sleep is kind of like peeing. They look at me in surprise (*Why is this grown-up talking about peeing?!*), and I ask, "What would happen if I decided, 'I'm never going to pee, ever again!'" Eventually, the body does what it needs to do. The same is true with sleep. I tell kids, "You don't need to worry about getting enough sleep. As long as you get enough rest—which means lying quietly with your eyes closed—you will get enough sleep. Maybe not tonight, maybe not tomorrow night, but pretty soon, your body will sort things out." I also emphasize that feeling tired can be unpleasant, but it's not dangerous.

Then we talk about fun things to think about while waiting to fall asleep. This might include planning their next birthday, remembering a fun family vacation, or imagining being a character in their favorite book, movie, or TV show.

Learning to Choose

Many children with low self-esteem struggle to make even simple decisions. They don't trust their own judgment, so they fret about the possibility of making a wrong choice, or they even refuse to choose. But making decisions is an important part of finding their own voice. Teaching your child about the decision-making process can help.

Bust These Myths About Decision Making

One reason that children with low self-esteem have such a hard time choosing is that they have mistaken beliefs about what is needed to make decisions. Here are some common myths about decision making, along with the truth behind the myths. See if your child can explain why the myths aren't true.

- **Myth:** *I must be 100 percent certain in order to make a decision.*

  Truth: Nothing in life is 100 percent certain.

- **Myth:** *In order to make a decision, I must analyze things endlessly.*

  Truth: At some point, further thought or discussion doesn't improve the quality of the decision.

- **Myth:** *Making a decision should be easy (and I'm stupid if I can't decide).*

  Truth: Sometimes it's easy to decide; sometimes it isn't. The difficulty depends on the type of decision and how much practice you've had making decisions.

- **Myth:** *I must be completely happy with my choice.*

  Truth: Choosing one option means letting go of other options. It's common to have mixed feelings about a decision.

- **Myth:** *If I make a wrong choice, it will be unbearable.*

  Truth: If you make a wrong choice, you will feel disappointment and regret, but you will survive. You'll also probably learn something about yourself or the situation that can guide future decisions.

- **Myth:** *A perfect choice exists, and I can't decide until I've figured out what it is.*

  Truth: Most decisions are compromises or just reasonable guesses, based on whatever information is available at the time. If one choice turns out to be wrong, it doesn't mean the other choice was right. There are costs and benefits to most choices. What's right for one person may not be right for another person, and what seems right for you now may not be right for you later. All of this is okay. You'll adjust when and if you need to do so.

- **Myth:** *If I keep thinking and avoid deciding, I won't make a bad choice.*

  Truth: *Not deciding* is a choice. It's a choice to avoid taking action, to refuse commitment, and to react passively. It's a choice to stay mired in uncertainty and allow opportunities to pass. Not deciding is rarely a positive choice. It's living by default.

Visit http://www.newharbinger.com/40491 to download this list.

Practice Making Small Choices Quickly

Look for opportunities for your child to practice making small choices quickly. Ordering food, picking which shirt to buy or wear, choosing which game to play with you…these are all low-stakes decisions that your child can learn to make quickly. If your child struggles a great deal with decisions, you may want to pick only one type of decision to work on at first.

Explain that learning to decide quickly is a skill that takes practice to master. Offer your child some possible strategies for making quick decisions. These include

- Going with your first instinct.

- Flipping a coin.

- Saying "Eenie-meenie-minie-mo."

- Choosing the option that comes first in the alphabet.

- Closing your eyes and pointing to one.

If your child dithers about which strategy to try, then for one week use flipping a coin to make quick small decisions. After a week, your child can try a different decision-making strategy or stick with the coin flip. Once your child has made a quick choice, stick with it. Whether or not your child feels happy with the choice afterward, he will eventually learn that it's possible to make choices quickly and that disappointment is bearable. By making decisions quickly, your child is choosing freedom from the misery of indecision.

Learn Constructive Approaches to Bigger Decisions

In addition to learning strategies for quick decisions, your child may benefit from learning how to think constructively about bigger decisions. Here are some ideas:

Eliminate options. Classic research shows that having too many options can be overwhelming and make people not want to make any choice (Iyengar and Lepper 2000). Although more recent research shows that *choice overload* doesn't always happen with a greater number of options (Scheibehenne, Greifeneder, and Todd 2009), eliminating possibilities can be an excellent way to simplify decisions. Encourage your child to figure out which options are "definite nos." Once an option is eliminated, it's gone for good for that particular decision at that time. Don't let your child bring it back into consideration. Narrow the focus on the remaining options.

List pros and cons. Listing pros and cons is a tried-and-true decision-making strategy. Putting thoughts to paper can also help minimize the pointless circles of rumination. This method also highlights that no option is perfect.

Talk to someone who is already doing what you're considering doing. Our imagination isn't always a good guide to how we'll feel in different circumstances. As Daniel Gilbert (2006) points out, we tend to overlook certain possibilities and overemphasize others. How we feel now affects how we imagine we'll feel in the future, and negative outcomes usually don't end up feeling as bad as we imagine they will. According to Gilbert, the best way to get around these limitations of imagination and predict whether we would be happy doing something is to ask someone who is already doing it. Your child may feel comfortable asking a classmate, relative, or neighbor about the possible choice. Alternatively, you may need to help your child find an appropriate person to ask. If there's no other option, you could ask parents about their children's experiences and share the information with your child.

Try self-polling. One of my favorite strategies when I have a big decision to make is to poll myself repeatedly. I ask myself, "If I had to pick right this second, what would I choose?" I can poll myself again five minutes later and maybe get a different result, but over time, a pattern emerges showing that I lean toward one option more than others.

Set a time limit. Ask your child how much time a particular decision is worth. If she isn't sure, ask how much time most kids would spend trying to make this decision. If your child still doesn't know, you may need to set a time limit. Making decisions can be challenging, but it definitely shouldn't involve endless suffering. Before the time limit, your child can gather information or weigh options, but once the decision time arrives, a choice must be made. If your child insists she still can't decide, use one of the quick-decision techniques and be done. It's usually better to make an imperfect decision than to wallow in indecision.

Explain That the Right Answer Isn't "Out There"

The most compelling discussion of choice I've come across is Ruth Chang's work on "how to make hard choices" (Chang 2017). If you have an older child, you may want to listen to her inspiring fifteen-minute TED talk together. Chang explains that in hard choices, there is no clear best alternative, because the options differ in multiple and important ways. A hard choice is like comparing an apple to an orange. Neither one is obviously better than the other, because they are so different. Hard choices are difficult, not because we're too stupid to know the correct answer but because we expect the answer to be "out there." Chang thrillingly argues that through hard choices we make ourselves who we are. We don't just logically weigh facts; we create our own reasons for hard choices and effectively declare *This is who I am! This is what I'm for!* Seen from this perspective, hard choices aren't about being right; they're about creating our selves.

Taking Action

Choices are ultimately about taking action. Children with low self-esteem often don't try to solve problems, because they're convinced there's no hope. Here are some ideas for helping your child move beyond passive helplessness and avoidance.

Have Faith in Your Child's Growing Ability to Cope

When kids say, "I can't! It's too hard!" it's tempting to leap to the rescue. It's hard to see a child we love suffering, especially when we know we could easily fix things.

But when we step in to solve problems that our children could solve on their own, we steal their opportunity to develop important coping skills. When we say, "I'll call his mom," "I'll email the teacher," or "I'll take care of it," the message we give our kids is *You can't handle this!* As children move through the elementary school years, they increasingly view parental help as a sign that they are incompetent (Pomerantz and Eaton 2000).

We want our children to have a sense of agency, to know that they can intentionally take action to influence what's happening around them. They can't get this through sitting passively on the sidelines. They won't get it through hearing "You can do it!" pep talks that have nothing to do with their experience. They also won't get it by constantly failing in the face of excessive demands.

Learning to cope requires many experiences of trying and succeeding, struggling and overcoming. As parents, we need to use our judgment to find that sweet spot where our kids feel challenged but not overwhelmed by the problems they face. We can coach and comfort, rehearse and encourage, but we want to support our children's ability to take action by handling problems on their own. That's the only way they can come to see themselves as capable.

Focus on Collaborative Problem Solving

Kids with low self-esteem tend to get derailed with problem solving, because they're quick to dismiss all alternatives, saying "Nothing will work!" They'd rather avoid dealing with problems than make a decision or take action. I'm a big fan of Ross Greene's

(2016) gentle and collaborative approach to problem solving. Here's a brief summary:

Step 1: Offer empathy. Greene recommends that parents bring up a problem by saying "I've noticed..." and describe the troubling situation or behavior you've observed. Then ask, "What's up?" In this step, parents should be genuinely curious about the child's experiences, thoughts, and feelings. Keep summarizing, acknowledging, and asking who-what-when-where questions to thoroughly understand your child's perspective on the problem.

Step 2: Define adult concern. Instead of rushing in with suggestions, parents need to gently broach the issue by explaining how the problem is negatively affecting the child or others. Greene suggests starting with the phrase "My concern is..."

Step 3: Invite your child to problem-solve. In this step, parents invite kids to come up with possible solutions that address both the child's concerns and the parent's concerns. Greene recommends saying "I wonder if there's a way to [address child's concern] and [address parent's concern]?" Another way to say this is to summarize the problem in terms of the different concerns, "So, on the one hand [child's concern] and on the other hand [parent's concern]." Then parents can ask, "Do you have any ideas about what we can do?"

In the third step, if your child suggests something unreasonable, don't get sucked into an argument! Just say, "Well, that's one option, but it doesn't take care of the part about [fill in the blank]. Let's see if we can come up with something that works for both of us. What else could we try?"

If your child comes up with a possible solution, ask questions to help your child flesh it out. Anticipate different circumstances and possible obstacles ("What if...?" "What about when...?"), and see if your child can come up with plans for addressing these.

Keep working together until you come up with a plan that is realistic and addresses both of your concerns. If the two of you don't immediately come up with a solution, that's okay. Tell your child, "Let's think about this some more and talk again later."

This whole sequence can seem daunting at first, but with practice kids definitely get faster at doing it. And it's such important work! This kind of problem solving gently pulls kids with low self-esteem out of their passive brooding. It gives them a chance to articulate their concerns in a very specific and actionable way, broadens their perspective beyond their self-focus on their misery and flaws, and helps them to take positive action in a supportive context. And when their solutions work—even partially—they can begin to feel less helpless and more capable.

Think Through How to Speak Up

Children with low self-esteem wallow helplessly or fume silently, because they think people either won't listen or will get mad at them if they ask for what they want. Eventually, their brewing resentment may spill out in angry accusations. When others respond negatively to their explosion, they conclude, *I knew it wouldn't help to talk about it!*

I had a client once, an elementary school girl, who felt hurt because her friend was sitting with another friend on the bus. She stewed about this for quite a while, then decided to write a long letter to the other girl, telling her how mean she was. Needless to say, the other girl didn't respond well. She definitely didn't say, "Ooh! Your mean letter has inspired me to want to sit next to you from now on!"

Before speaking up, your child should consider these questions:

1. *What will happen if I say nothing?*

   Will the situation continue? Will it get worse? Will your child's resentment grow? Resentment is poison in any relationship. Suffering in silence may seem like a nice thing to do, but it can destroy a friendship. Being able to imagine what will happen may motivate your child to act.

149

2. *Is this person someone who cares about what I want and how I feel?*

The harsh truth is that not everyone cares about your child's feelings. Your child is more likely to be successful speaking up to someone who does care. Although it's sometimes necessary to speak up to people who don't care about us, that's not the place to start for kids who struggle to find their voice. It's easier to speak up to someone who is likely to be receptive.

3. *What specifically do I want the other person to do?*

Being able to think about desired outcomes in specific and concrete ways can help children articulate what they want. For example, thinking *Everyone should stop always being mean to me* doesn't suggest a path forward, but realizing *I want them to take turns being It* or *I want her to ask before borrowing my eraser* or *I want him to include me in the group project* is an actionable goal.

4. *How does the other person view this situation?*

The ability to imagine someone else's perspective is an emerging skill for children. As parents, we can play an important role in helping our kids develop this ability. We can ask questions such as "What are some reasons she might have done that (besides trying to be mean)?" "How do you think he's likely to react if you say that?" or "How would you feel if someone said that to you?" Perspective-taking questions help children see beyond their own upset to consider other people's needs and wishes. That's essential for building relationships.

5. *How can I communicate what I want so that others can hear it?*

Children don't necessarily know what to say to convey what they want. Stating their own wishes and feelings with *I-statements* and focusing on moving forward are both essential to effective communication.

Role-play can be very useful for gaining confidence in speaking up. Here are some useful phrases you can practice with your child. Have your child mix and match, creating statements that combine one phrase from each column.

I-Statement	Desired Action
"I want to…"	"How about if we…?"
"I don't like…"	"Let's…"
"I'd rather…"	"I want to…"
"I think…"	"From now on, could you please…?"
"I feel…"	"Can I…?"
"I like…"	"Will you…?"

For example, if your child is tired of always being It in a game of tag, a good way to say this to a friend could be "I don't like being It all the time. How about if we do eenie-meenie-minie-mo to decide who's It today?" Clear communication doesn't guarantee that other people will go along with what your child wants, but it's much more likely to be effective than passive brooding or angry accusations.

Teach Your Child to Ask for Help the Right Way

Everyone needs help sometimes, but children with low self-esteem have trouble asking for it. They either refuse to ask for help, because they're embarrassed about needing it, or whine helplessly, insisting repeatedly that they just can't do something, which can be annoying to others.

Here's a better approach that children can use to ask for help: first, list two strategies they've used to try to solve the problem; then ask for the specific type of help they want.

For example, if your child doesn't understand a math assignment, a good way to ask the teacher for help might involve saying "I tried looking at the example problem and reading the textbook, but I still don't understand how to do these problems. Could you please show me?" Mentioning the two attempted strategies shows that your child isn't giving up instantly. Asking for a specific type of help makes it more likely that your child will get the desired response.

Focus on the Next Step

Children with low self-esteem become easily overwhelmed when they think about facing challenges or solving problems. They imagine everything they'll have to do on the whole journey, and it seems easier just to do nothing. They want the demands and expectations to just disappear, because they can't imagine themselves being able to do everything that's required.

If your child seems stuck like this, focus on building momentum. Help your child come up with just one tiny step, one small change that doesn't seem too hard, in order to break through inertia.

Kids with low self-esteem are quick to object, "But if I do that, they'll expect more!" Keep your child focused on now. Say, "If it becomes too much, we'll deal with that when and if it happens. What's the next step? That's all you need to focus on."

What if your child says, "But I don't feel ready!" Ask your child, "What would make you feel more ready?" Probably nothing.

The best writing advice I ever got is "Start before you feel ready." The truth is that most of the time we're not fully ready to deal with whatever we have to deal with, but we do it anyway.

Encourage your child to embrace discovery—to try, then adjust. We don't have to be completely ready or certain before we try, but we'll definitely know more after trying than we did while we were just waiting. And it's much easier to keep going once we start.

Wrap-Up

If your child has a tendency to get stuck in a pattern of indecision and passive helplessness, developing real self-esteem will require lots of guidance and practice learning to make choices without getting tangled up by self-doubt. You can teach your child to recognize unproductive rumination and to use various decision-making strategies. The most important thing your child needs to learn is that the right answers aren't "out there." Your child creates the right answers by choosing and doing.

The next chapter will look at children who feel like outsiders because they're different from their peers, which can have a huge impact on self-esteem.

Take-Home Points

- Children with low self-esteem tend to ruminate, which means going over and over negative thoughts.

- Rumination compounds misery, intensifies low self-esteem, and gets in the way of coping.

- Although children with low self-esteem struggle to make choices, doing so is an important part of finding their own voice.

- Children with low self-esteem need a sense of agency, which involves intentionally taking action to influence what's happening around them.

"I Don't Fit In!"

When Your Child Struggles with Feeling Different

Mr. Ricardo, the school counselor, sat across from Adam. "So, Adam, you've been at our school for a month, now. How's it going?"

"Fine," Adam answered blandly.

"Have you made friends?"

"I dunno."

"I noticed you were sitting alone at lunch today."

"Uh-huh."

"It can be hard to find your place in a new school," Mr. Ricardo said gently.

"I don't belong here. I just don't fit in," Adam insisted.

"What do you mean?"

"I'm not an athlete, so I don't fit in with the boys in my class who like sports. I don't like video games, so I don't fit in with those kids either. Plus I'm fat, and I have stupid freckles...I don't fit in with anyone."

"You're feeling like an outsider here. Was it like that at your old school?"

"Kind of," Adam said. "I guess I'm not the kind of kid other kids want to be around. I'm just different from everybody else."

Every child is unique. For some children, this can be a point of pride. For others, like Adam, being different makes them feel hopelessly disconnected and flawed. Feeling like an outsider is extremely painful. In fact, there's evidence that the brain responds to social rejection the same way it does to physical pain (Kross et al. 2011a).

From about third grade on, children begin to have a sense of how others, in general, view them, and this is strongly related to their overall self-esteem (Harter 2006)). In other words, how kids feel about themselves is closely linked to how they think other kids feel about them. In Adam's case, he believes he is unacceptable to his classmates, and he has a long list of reasons for this, including his abilities, his interests, and his appearance.

Feeling Different and Disconnected

There are a million reasons why kids might feel separate from their peers. Being other-than-typical in their community in terms of family structure or income, medical challenges, ethnic or religious background, sexual orientation, physical appearance, learning issues, and so on can give kids a sense that they are the odd one out. Sometimes the differences are subtle. Having interests, feelings, or experiences that aren't mainstream might be acutely prominent to a child but not necessarily apparent to other children or adults. On the other hand, sometimes the differences that make children feel separate can be spotted by anyone, from across the room.

In terms of self-esteem, what matters for children is the meaning that they attach to their differences. How much do these differences matter? Are they permanent or temporary? Are they central or peripheral to their sense of who they are? Are there benefits to having these differences? Do they think about them frequently or only occasionally? Do they see them as a cause of negative reactions from peers?

Children with low self-esteem often perceive themselves as not just different but also worse than their peers. They torture themselves with the idea, *If only I were* [fill in the blank], *other kids would like me, and my life would be perfect!* They may even believe, *Because I'm* [fill in the blank], *I'm unlikable and worthless, so there's no hope for me!*

The Self-Fulfilling Prophecy of Believing "I Don't Belong"

Adam was sitting by himself at lunch, convinced that there was no possibility of anyone liking him, so he didn't even try to reach out. This style of relating is called *anxious solitude* or *social withdrawal*. Children with this pattern of behavior get caught in a vicious cycle of worry, avoidance, and rejection. They want to belong, but they feel awkward and self-conscious. Because they feel uncomfortable around others, they avoid talking to or even being near their peers. To protect themselves from the rejection they expect, they cower at the edges of the group. They sit apart, spending most of their time playing alone or just silently watching other kids having fun together.

Unfortunately, their standoffishness sends the message to other children that they're not interested in connecting, so their peers ignore them. But having fewer social interactions also means they get less practice being around other kids, sharing fun times, and learning how to get along. If they do try to reach out, they're likely to do so clumsily, calling attention to themselves in ways that are off-putting to their peers and eliciting the rejection they fear. Because they expect to be rejected, they also tend to see even neutral reactions from peers as signs that they are unwanted. So they continue to avoid social situations. Other children treat them as if they were invisible, which makes them feel relieved (*Phew! No one's noticing me!*), worried (*What if someone says something mean to me?*), and heartbroken (*Why am I always the outsider?*). The cycle continues with these children wanting to connect but holding themselves back, day after day confirming their fear that they don't belong.

Not surprisingly, research tells us that children with the anxious withdrawal pattern of behavior are at risk for anxiety, depression, loneliness, and low self-esteem (Rubin, Coplan, and Bowker 2009). Like Adam, they blame their disconnection on what they see as their personal flaws (Wichmann, Coplan, and Daniels 2004). This makes them feel hopeless: how could anyone accept them when they're so different and inadequate?

Shifting the Narrative

Children like Adam believe that their differences are their main problem. While being different from peers can sometimes lead to peer rejection and even bullying (see chapter 10), constant and harshly self-critical focus on differences can also lead to feelings of inadequacy and get in the way of connecting with others.

At one level, feeling different is an issue of connection. These kids want to fit in with their peers. At another level, it's an issue of choice, because how children understand their differences reflects their values. Dealing with differences forces children to grapple with important questions about what they believe and what matters to them. When do they try to adapt to a group, and when do they choose to stand apart from a group or find a different group?

Real self-esteem for children like Adam means being able to put their differences in context, so they can embrace or at least accept them, rather than see them as an impenetrable wall permanently separating them from their peers. Different doesn't have to mean bad, worthless, or alone.

Real Self-Esteem Tips to Try

This chapter focuses on helping kids who feel like outsiders. It will talk about ways to address the meaning that children attach to their differences and challenge the mental yardstick they use for measuring their worth. It will also look specifically at concerns about appearance. Finally, it will discuss ways to help children who feel different find some form of community where they can feel like they belong.

Addressing the Meaning of Differences

Children are bombarded, through ads, news, social media, and daily interactions, by intentional and unintentional messages about what qualities are "normal" and socially desirable. They see overt prejudice and more subtle microaggressions. Omissions can speak as loudly as direct negative remarks. When kids don't see people who look, feel, or act like them on TV or in movies or books, they can feel invisible, overlooked, or devalued. Children pick up on all of these messages, and they make inferences about their own worth. Regardless of how society—or their classmates—reacts to their differences, children need to form their own views about what their differences mean to them.

There is no one answer when it comes to helping children deal with differences. The specific coping responses will vary depending on the type of difference involved. For example, children might feel like an outsider due to having diabetes, being in the "low" math group, being Jewish in a predominantly Christian school, or being overweight. However, all of these children need to find a workable answer to the question *What does it mean to me to be different from my peers?* We definitely don't want to trivialize or dismiss real differences or painful struggles with various forms of bias, but we also don't want kids to see themselves as one-dimensional characters with their differences as their defining feature. It's essential that children find some kind of context that allows them to move forward in healthy ways, acknowledging their differences without feeling isolated or diminished by them. Here are some strategies to try.

Let Your Child Educate the Class About Differences

People sometimes react negatively to what they don't understand. It may be helpful to arrange for your child to give a presentation to classmates about her difference. Help your child prepare answers to common questions and explain which responses from peers are or aren't helpful. For example, if your daughter has a peanut allergy, she could explain what this means, how she found out that she has it, what happens if she's exposed to peanuts, and how classmates can help keep her safe. This type of presentation can be empowering for a child who feels different, and it's likely to increase classmates' awareness and empathy.

Prepare for Rude Comments or Questions

If your child's difference is visible or somehow comes to the attention of classmates, other kids will probably comment on it. They're not necessarily trying to be mean. Kids are curious, and they may not realize how uncomfortable their remarks can make children with differences feel. For example, a classmate asked a client of mine whose father had died, "Why aren't you crying all the time? Don't you miss your dad?" Another client who wore hearing aids had to deal with frequent questions about "What are those things in your ears?" It's not just kids who can be rude about differences. A client of mine has a relative who uses a wheelchair and is often asked by adults out in public whether they can take his picture. Many children report hearing rude comments with the tagline "No offense, but…"

It will be easier for your child to handle these situations if you've already rehearsed some answers. How your child responds will depend on the context and the relationship. Answers can range from brief explanations ("Those are my hearing aids. They help me hear better") to a noncommittal shrug or "Hmmm…" to clear assertion or limit setting ("I don't like it when you touch my hair, so please don't") to direct confrontation ("That's a rude question"), then walking away.

Beware of Blaming the Difference

Children who are acutely aware of feeling different may be quick to explain any negative event in terms of that difference. Their intense self-focus on the difference makes it feel very prominent for them, so they assume it's also very prominent for others. They may even be on the lookout for signs that people are rejecting them because of their differences. They may say things like "She hates me because I wear glasses" or "They left me out because I'm the only one with a classroom aide" or "He said that because he knows I'm gay." Maybe. But not necessarily.

If this sounds like your child, don't argue directly by saying "I'm sure that's not the case!" Your child will just insist more loudly that it is. Instead, acknowledge that possibility but also see if your child can come up with other possible explanations that don't involve the difference. You could point out, "Maybe the fact that she doesn't like you has nothing to do with your glasses. Maybe she was just temporarily annoyed because you got picked to be line leader and she didn't," or "Maybe they didn't realize you wanted to be included. They were just having fun and didn't notice that you were there," or even "Maybe he's a jerk to everyone, and his comment says more about him than you."

Promote Pride and Prepare for Prejudice

Promoting group pride by teaching children about their race, culture, or ethnicity can be a powerful way to help them see differences in a positive context. Various studies have found that 85 percent of Puerto Rican parents, 80 percent of African-American parents, and 66 percent of Japanese-American parents report teaching their children about their cultural heritage, history, and traditions (Hughes et al. 2006). The stories we tell our children about where they come from help them feel connected to their ancestors, their broader family, and others of their background.

For children in ethnic, racial, or religious minority groups, learning about their background often comes hand in hand with learning about bias. Bias can be blatant or subtle and even unconscious. One study of white North American children and adults found that a rapid association task involving pictures and words revealed equivalent levels of implicit or automatic pro-white/anti-black attitudes in six-year-olds, ten-year-olds, and adults. However, only the youngest children explicitly reported anti-black views. The older children claimed they were less biased, and the adults insisted that they were not biased at all in their racial attitudes (Baron and Banaji 2006). (For a fascinating look at your own or your older child's implicit stereotypes, involving thoughts and feelings outside of conscious awareness and control, visit the website for Harvard University's Project Implicit.)

The ability to perceive discrimination can be an essential survival skill for minority children, who might otherwise blame themselves for hateful messages or practices they encounter. About 95 percent of African-American parents report having discussed discrimination with their children, helping them to be aware of it and prepare to cope with it. In contrast, only 10 percent of immigrant Chinese parents say they discuss bias with their children, perhaps reflecting cultural values related to maintaining harmony.

About two-thirds of parents from African-American, white, and Latino backgrounds say they encourage their children to focus on individual qualities, such as hard work, virtue, and egalitarian values, that can help them thrive in the dominant culture, whereas only about one-fifth of Japanese-American parents report promoting egalitarianism. Encouraging color-blindness to race was a prominent strategy only among white parents (Hughes et al. 2006; Marks et al. 2015). You're the best judge of what strategies make the most sense for your family and your child, given your particular circumstances.

Look for Inspiring Examples

Children with low self-esteem often believe they are the only ones with their particular challenges. Learning about famous people who share your child's difference and have thrived can be very inspiring. For example, you might want to help your child identify and maybe even read biographies of or watch movies about famous people with high-functioning autism, famous African-American scientists, or famous athletes with physical disabilities.

Extended family members can sometimes be inspiring examples, but tread carefully. To be effective, the model has to be someone your child both admires and feels similar to. Otherwise, a comparison could create resentment by implying *Your [cousin/brother/father] is doing extremely well, despite this difference. So, what's wrong with you? Why can't you be more like him?* That will make your child feel either more inadequate or more determined to be nothing like the shining example.

Handling Appearance-Related Concerns

At all ages, satisfaction with their physical appearance is the largest predictor of children's self-esteem (Harter 2015). From fourth grade onwards, compared to boys, girls are noticeably and increasingly more dissatisfied with their appearance. Being different from peers in terms of body weight can be especially painful for children. Sadly, children's perceptions that other kids respond negatively to their physical differences may be accurate. Even preschoolers believe that peers with larger bodies have negative traits (Su and Di Santo 2012). By elementary school, unkind stereotypes about children who are overweight are common. The heavier children are, the more likely they are to be victimized by their peers (Lumeng et al. 2010).

In the broader culture, bias against overweight people is both widespread and widely tolerated. Obesity is a complicated issue with multiple causes, but popular culture often characterizes it as a moral failing. Fat is often described as "disgusting," and there's a common assumption that being shamed will motivate people to lose weight. The truth is that shame doesn't inspire positive change; it just contributes to helplessness, isolation, and more unhealthy habits (Pont et al. 2017).

Too often, children internalize these harsh messages and hate themselves because of their weight. According to Common Sense Media (2015), over half of girls and a third of boys ages six to eight think they ought to be thinner than they are. By age seven, one out of four children has tried some form of dieting.

First Acknowledge Rather Than Try to Fix Problems

When our children are hurting, we adults tend to want to go straight to active problem-solving mode. That might be useful later, but it's not where we should start. A child who feels flawed and disconnected from peers needs strong connection at home.

So, if your daughter comes to you and says something like "I feel fat," don't leap to plan an exercise program or launch into a lecture on the fact that *fat* is not a feeling. Or, if your son complains that he's embarrassed about having acne or about being shorter than his peers, don't shift the focus to how mean the other kids are. Slow down. Listen. Let your child feel your understanding and unconditional acceptance before broaching any ideas of what to do.

You might begin by saying "You seem upset. What's going on?" Then focus on describing your child's thoughts or feelings. Depending on what the issue is, you could respond to your child by saying something like "It hurt your feelings when he said that," "You're mad that they treated you that way," "It feels unfair to you that you have to work so hard to keep track of your insulin levels, and other kids get to eat without thinking," or just "It's hard when that happens." If you're not sure how to respond, simply echo what your child said, so that she feels heard. You may need to make several of these comments until your child begins to settle, knowing that you get it.

At some point, you may want to ask, "Do you need a hug?" If it was a particularly painful day, your child may even cry in your arms.

Afterward, when your child seems calmer, you can ask, "What do you think might help?" Or, if the situation is something that can't easily be fixed, you may just want to suggest hanging out and doing something enjoyable together. Your understanding and comfort matter.

Develop Your Child's Media Literacy

Boys as well as girls are concerned with falling short of how they "ought" to look. We can't completely protect our children from being exposed to dehumanizing and impossible physical standards, but we can help them learn to recognize, analyze, and evaluate advertising and media messages. A quick online search for "photoshopped images of models" could inspire an interesting discussion with your child about what advertisers change in photos and why. Make a game of spotting fake images so that your child is less susceptible to being influenced by these unrealistic depictions. You can also challenge the idea that bodies are primarily decorative rather than strong and useful.

You may want to talk about how certain groups of people are portrayed in movies and on TV. Children ages nine and up may be interested in contrasting media that offer positive, empowering, and realistic portrayals with those that perpetuate stereotypes.

Make thoughtful choices about what kinds of media you allow in your home. Common Sense Media offers in-depth analyses of the content of movies, TV shows, books, and electronic games, so you can figure out what's right for your family. Show these reviews to your child and talk about why you think certain media are or aren't appropriate.

Don't be shy about communicating your family's values. You can say, "In our family, we believe…" "In our family, we think what matters most is…" "In our family, we care about…" Then explain why. Personal or family stories related to these values may make them especially vivid and memorable for your child.

Look at the Whole Package

Children with low self-esteem tend to focus on parts of themselves rather than the whole. They look with microscopic intensity at their flaws, without seeing them in the context of a complete person.

One way to address this is to help your child understand that looking too closely distorts perception. Choose any photo on a computer, and zoom in until the photo is an indecipherable mess of blobs of color. Now see if your child can guess what the picture is. Your child won't be able to tell until you zoom out enough that the tiny blobs combine to make a whole. Make the point that zeroing in on one tiny aspect of your child is no more useful or accurate than focusing on one tiny gray blob in the photo. Sure, it's there, but it's the whole picture that matters.

Another way of encouraging a holistic view is to connect your child's differences to people your child cares about. Rather than denying or dismissing differences, you could say, for example, "Yep, that's how we grow 'em in our family. We get the round hips *and* also the math skills" or "Yes, ADHD runs in our family *and* so do quick reflexes and creativity. It's a package deal."

Treat Their Body Kindly

Children who hate how they look sometimes take a punitive stance toward their bodies. They deliberately dress in old, baggy, unattractive clothes or stuff themselves into clothing that no longer fits, because that's the size they think they should be. They may also try harsh strategies to try to lose weight, such as skipping meals or creating unrealistically ambitious exercise plans. When they fall short on these inhumane plans, they hate themselves more.

You need to intervene directly to promote a kinder and gentler approach to their body. For the vast majority of children, dieting to lose weight is not appropriate. Emphasize healthy choices. Make this a family-wide goal and focus on changing just one small habit at a time. For example, you might try taking a walk together after dinner, signing up for a fun physical activity, or having a healthy snack after school.

Insist on appropriate hygiene: showering, brushing teeth, tending hair, and wearing clothes that don't smell. That's all part of taking care of our bodies.

In terms of clothing, help your child pick colors or styles that he likes and feels comfortable in. Your child doesn't have to be the most fashionable kid in school or wear the most expensive sneakers, but dressing in comfortable and attractive clothes is a way for children to treat their body kindly. Get rid of anything that doesn't fit your child. Overly tight clothes can be a symbol of inadequacy for your child.

Helping Your Child Find a Tribe

In addition to putting their differences in context, children who feel disconnected from their peers need to find their tribe: a group of peers where they feel they belong. As parents, we think of our children as individuals, so the idea of our children being part of a group can be uncomfortable. Some parents even say, "I want my child to be unique!" or "I want my child to be a leader, not a follower!" Finding a tribe is not about turning into a copy of everyone else. It's about thoughtfully choosing and contributing to a community. In order to lead, children first need to be able to join. The right community helps kids feel connected and valued. It embraces rather than erases uniqueness.

Social Groups vs. One-On-One Friendships

Social groups, or cliques, usually consist of three to ten children who choose to be together and see themselves as similar. Social groups are related to one-on-one-friendships, because kids are likely to be in groups with their individual friends, but they're a different aspect of children's social lives. (See chapter 5 for a discussion of one-on-one friendships). Children in a social group aren't necessarily all friends with each other, but they spend free time together. Groups offer a whole new dimension of fun, support, and belonging. They can also be a safety net for weathering ups and downs in individual friendships.

Although social groups can form as early as preschool, they become increasingly important as children get older. Among first and second graders, about half are part of a social group (Witvliet et al. 2010). By fourth grade, almost all children (97 percent) hang around with a group of kids as either a central or a peripheral member (Bagwell et al. 2000). By seventh grade, over 75 percent of children mostly hang out with one or more groups of friends. Less than 15 percent of seventh graders mostly hang out with a single friend, and less than 10 percent mostly hang out with "no one in particular" (Crockett, Losoff, and Peterson 1984).

A fascinating study by Miranda Witvliet and her colleagues (2010) looked at changes in social group membership of first graders over the course of a year. They found that children who were members of a social group were, according to classmates and teachers, kinder, happier, and better liked by peers than those who had only one-on-one friendships. Those with one-on-one friendships were, in turn, better adjusted than those who had no friends. Surprisingly, the children with only one-on-one friendships were more similar in well-being to the kids with no friends than to the social group members.

Between first and second grade, roughly half of all children in the study changed their type of friendship, mostly moving only one step up or down the scale of social involvement. For instance, among the children who started as part of a social group, 65 percent were still in a group a year later, while 30 percent moved to having just one-on-one-friendships, and 5 percent became friendless. Among the children who started with one-on-one-friendships, 45 percent continued to have one-on-one friendships, 40 percent joined a social group, and only 15 percent became isolated. The hopeful news for friendless children is that, over the course of the year, 39 percent gained a one-on-one friend, and 22 percent moved into a social group.

Drawbacks of Social Groups

Although being part of a social group can be both fun and comforting for kids, there are some complications related to influence, exclusivity, and status. Let's look at each of these complications.

Group members *influence* each other. Children are initially drawn to form social groups with others whom they perceive to be like them. Over time, group norms or expectations emerge about how members generally think and behave, and members of a social group become even more similar. Children are motivated to conform to group norms because they want to remain part of the group. This means that the attitudes and behavior of the members can determine whether the group influence is positive or negative. If your child is hanging out with kids who care about academics, this could inspire more studying. On the other hand, socializing with kids who don't care about school could have a negative impact on your child's study habits. Beyond academics, social group members also tend to become more alike over time in their level of kindness, aggression, rule breaking, and social withdrawal. The more cohesive the group, the stronger the influence (Ellis and Zarbatany 2017).

Another complication of social groups has to do with their *exclusivity*. By definition, a social group implies that some people are included as members of the group ("us"), and some are not ("them"). Children like members of their own social group, whom they see as similar to them, more than they like those who are outside the group and dissimilar to them. They regard these *in-group members* as having more positive traits, prefer being with them, and favor them when sharing resources (Killen, Mulvey, and Hitti 2013; Kwon, Lease, and Hoffman 2012). In-group preferences occur even when children are divided into groups based on meaningless criteria, such as randomly receiving a blue or a yellow T-shirt (Bigler, Brown, and Markell 2001).

Unfortunately, sometimes in-group preferences can turn into dislike or even hatred of outsiders. Clever experiments involving leading children to believe that they are part of an imaginary team and then manipulating what they believe "other people on your team" think have shown that group norms can influence how children respond to outsiders. Children tend to like people outside their social group when their group has a norm of being fair and friendly to outsiders, but not when the in-group norm is to dislike outsiders (Nesdale 2011). Having a common enemy can increase solidarity and make in-group members feel superior, but prejudice against children who are different isn't what most parents want as the basis for their children's sense of belonging. Fortunately, children's increasing ability to engage in moral reasoning can help counter in-group biases, as they learn to temper their wish to support their group identity with their desire to do what's right by being kind and fair to those outside the group (Killen, Mulvey, and Hitti 2013; Rutland, Killen, and Abrams 2010).

A third complication related to social groups involves the issue of *status*. There is often one "popular" group that other children perceive as more socially dominant than other groups. It's common for children to be attracted to the idea of being a member of the popular group. However, popular children aren't necessarily well-liked by their peers (see chapter 5). They can be very aggressive and manipulative in trying to maintain or increase their status (Cillessen and Mayeux 2004a). It can also take a lot of time and energy to maintain a position in the popular group because of the constant pressure to be attractive, cool, and in-the-know. Research tells us that there are risks attached to being part of the popular group. Because they want to come across as edgy and interesting, kids in this group are more likely to get involved in drugs, alcohol, and early sexual activity (Schwartz and Hopmeyer Gorman 2011).

These three complications—influence, exclusivity, and status—mean that we need to help our children make wise choices when it comes to social groups. We want to guide them toward kind, healthy, and supportive groups where they can truly belong. We want our kids to form real connections, based on shared interests and activities, and we can help them do this.

Distinguish Between Fitting in and Belonging

In her book, *Daring Greatly*, Brené Brown (2015) makes an important distinction between just fitting in and truly belonging. She writes, "Fitting in is one of the greatest barriers to belonging. Fitting in is about assessing a situation and becoming who you need to be in order to be accepted. Belonging, on the other hand, doesn't require us to change who we are; it requires us to be who we are" (231–32). Belonging is about feeling known, accepted, and valued. Because children's sense of identity is only emerging and continuously growing, it's especially important that they be thoughtful about the company they keep. Here are some questions to help your child figure out whether or not a particular social group is a good fit:

- What do you have in common with them?

- How do you feel when you're with them?

- To what extent do you feel like you have to hide or change what you think or do to be accepted by them?

- Do they seem interested in what you think or feel, or do their opinions seem to matter more than yours?

- Can you relax around them, or do you feel like you have to be careful of what you say or do?

- Do you find yourself pretending around them?

- Do they bring out the best or the worst in you?

- When you make a mistake or do something that's not perfect, how do they respond?

- If you were upset about something, how would they react?

- How do the people in this group usually treat each other?

- How do they treat people who are not in this group?

- Do you like who you are when you're with them?

Visit http://www.newharbinger.com/40491 to download this list of questions.

Look for Team Experiences, Not Necessarily Sports

Because children's worlds are small, they often believe, *I'm the only one who...* Getting involved in various types of team experiences gives kids opportunity to feel part of something bigger than themselves. Sports teams can be great for creating a sense of belonging, but they are certainly not the only type of team. You may have to look beyond the school community to help your child find the right group. Possibilities include joining a choir, learning fencing, signing up for a robotics club, becoming active in a religious group, seeking out a diabetes support group, going to summer camp, or spending more time with cousins. The group may be related to your child's difference or it may allow your child to express or develop an interest unrelated to the difference. The goal is to have your child walk in the room and think, *Here are people like me!*

Urge Your Child to Start the Fun

Too often kids sit around feeling dejected and lonely because no one is inviting them to do things. The remedy could be for your child to be the one to issue the invitation. This will likely be scary for your child. It's hard to put ourselves out there! But the alternative is staying lonely.

One-on-one get-togethers are wonderful for deepening friend-ships (see chapter 5), but there's a special excitement and camarade-rie that comes from doing something as part of a group. Brainstorm with your child to come up with some possible activities to do with three or more kids. This could include going bowling, playing laser tag, meeting at a park, seeing a movie, or going out for pizza. Start with a relatively short event (up to two hours) to make it more likely that the get-together ends on a high note.

Once you've settled on an event, talk with your child about which kids might be willing to do this together. They don't have to be soul mates—just kids your child knows and has had friendly interactions with.

For younger children, you can call, text, or email the other parents to set up the event. If your child is in third grade or older, the invitation should probably come from her rather than you. A group text or email might be an easy way to do this. Help your child create the message to be sure it contains necessary details about location, date, time, and transportation. Send the message three to five days before the event. Plans are more likely to work if parents have some advance notice. If necessary, you can follow up with them after a day or two.

What if everyone says no? That's a possibility, but choosing an appealing activity and inviting enough kids (focusing on those who are kind and have been friendly with your child) will make it more likely that some say yes. Even if everyone is busy, your child will have done a good thing by reaching out. It's empowering for your child to practice inviting people and flattering for the other children to get invited. Also, the invitation could make other kids think of your child the next time they plan something.

Whether or not the outing happens, have your child wait two or three weeks before issuing another invitation to the same kids. This gives the other children a chance to reciprocate. In the meantime, your child could try inviting another group of kids.

Put Social Media in Perspective

Younger and younger children are becoming involved in social media. For those whose low self-esteem is related to feeling different, this can amplify feelings of disconnection and inadequacy. It's easy for kids to look at social media and believe that everyone else is amazingly beautiful, incredibly popular, and living a riotously exciting life. The contrast between what they see other kids doing online and their own ordinary lives can make them more focused on their flaws.

Social media can also heighten self-focus when children get caught up in building *streaks* and seeking *followers* or *likes* as a measure of their worth. They may spend excessive time trying to create perfect posts, obsessively checking how many people have responded, and fretting if people don't publicly approve their posts. But followers and likes are not the same as genuine relationships. Looking at these metrics tends to compound self-focus, self-judgment, approval seeking, and comparisons—all of which fuel low self-esteem.

I strongly encourage you to delay, delay, delay allowing your child to get a phone with Internet access or to use social media. Children, by definition, lack perspective. They just haven't been around that long or seen much of the world. Delaying gives your child time to grow up without the pressure of self-promotion. Even adults have trouble managing their time on and reactions to social media. It's a thousand times harder for kids.

When you do decide to let your child get a mobile phone or participate in social media, make it clear that there will be time limits, and you will do spot inspections to be sure your child is using the tool appropriately. Collect your child's cell phone or other electronic gadgets at bedtime. Nothing good ever happens on phones in the middle of the night.

You will definitely want to have a conversation with your child about healthy and unhealthy ways of being involved in social media.

It can be fun to share online and to see what friends post, but it's important for children to remember that social media is curated. People choose their best picture and most interesting activities to post. Some spend a lot of time modifying and perfecting their posts to look cooler than they really are. The single manufactured image they post represents one tiny moment, and we don't see the other 99.9 percent of their lives, filled with very ordinary moments. I often tell my clients, "You can't compare your inside to somebody else's outside."

When kids have the possibility of being electronically connected to their friends all the time, they need to think carefully about when they want to be disconnected. You can broach this topic by asking your child questions, such as "When would being on your phone get in the way of you focusing on or enjoying what you're doing?" "What do you think is reasonable in terms of how quickly people should respond to a text?" and "What information do you want to keep private?" Children need to be reminded that no electronic communications are private. They can easily be captured or forwarded. Tell your child, "Don't put anything online or in a text that you wouldn't want announced over morning announcements at your school."

You may also want to talk with your child about the fact that social media is run by companies whose business model is to get users to create the content for free (rather than paying writers or photographers), and they encourage people to stay on the site a long time and check it often so that they will be exposed to a lot of ads. From the company's perspective, getting kids hooked on social media is good business. Your child may even know of kids who use social media excessively.

Beware of Trying to Buy Acceptance

Sometimes when children feel like they don't fit in, they focus on materialistic goals to compensate, prove their worth, or project a certain image. Maybe a part of them believes that if they dress fashionably enough or own the coolest electronics, other kids will want to include them. This strategy is unlikely to work. As discussed in chapter 5, trying to impress peers is not the same as connecting with them. A study of fifth through twelfth graders found that children who endorsed questionnaire items such as "I like to own things that impress other people" and "My life would be better if I owned things I don't have right now" also reported worse self-esteem, lower happiness, and greater anxiety compared to kids who were less materialistic (Kasser 2005). We can't tell whether the materialism caused the low self-esteem, the low self-esteem caused the materialism, or both were caused by some other variable. Nevertheless, it's important to talk with your child about the issue of buying things to try to feel worthy. Ask your child how long the high of a recent purchase lasted. How long were other people interested in what they'd bought? What, if anything, in their life changed after the purchase? Do they even remember what you gave them for their birthday last year?

Encourage Service

When kids are focused on *What can I give?* they spend less mental energy on judging themselves for their differences. Volunteer work can be a great way to help your child feel meaningfully connected, as a valuable contributor to your community. Look especially for projects where a bunch of people have to pitch in together. Realizing *We did good!* is wonderfully bonding and empowering. Possible activities where kids can make a difference include regularly visiting older people in nursing homes, helping out at your local library or animal shelter, or pitching in with town cleanups.

Your child's guidance counselor may know of good opportunities at school. Maybe your child could help younger children practice reading or math or help them get their coats on when it's time to go home. Some schools have community gardens or composting programs that involve children of various ages.

Wrap-Up

Real self-esteem for kids who don't fit in involves seeing their differences in context, as part of who they are but not the whole story. You may need to help your child evaluate messages in popular culture about being different. Finding group experiences where your child can feel a sense of belonging is also important.

So far, this book has focused on the thoughts, feelings, and actions of children who don't like themselves for various reasons. However, we also need to look at the broader social context that these children find themselves in. Chapter 10 talks about ways to help children cope with bullying and other meanness from peers.

Take-Home Points

- Children need to form their own views about what their differences mean to them.

- Social media can heighten self-focus when children get caught up in building streaks and seeking followers or likes as a measure of their worth.

- Getting involved in various types of team and community-service experiences gives kids the opportunity to feel part of something bigger than themselves.

PART 5
THE BIGGER PICTURE

Coping with Bullying, Teasing, and Other Meanness

Too often, children with low self-esteem are picked on or bullied by other children. This is a chicken-and-egg situation. Meanness from peers can cause or contribute to low self-esteem, but low self-esteem can also make children easy targets for meanness.

Kids Are Often Mean

Meanness is common among children. For example, Debra Pepler and her colleagues (1998) video recorded the playground behavior of children in first through sixth grade whose teachers had identified them as either especially aggressive or especially nonaggressive. On average, the aggressive children did some form of mean behavior about every two minutes. But those carefully selected nonaggressive children averaged a mean behavior every three minutes!

Children are impulsive, their empathy and problem-solving skills aren't fully developed, and they often experiment with social power as they're learning to navigate the social world. All of these factors could lead kids to do mean things.

We adults haven't managed world peace or even perfect marriages, so it's unrealistic to think that kids will always be perfectly kind to each other. As parents, however, we can help our children cope with the meanness that they will inevitably encounter. And, even more important, we can try to guide them toward caring responses to their peers.

Distinguishing Between Bullying and Meanness

Bullying is more than just meanness. Researchers define *bullying* as deliberate cruelty, targeting a particular individual, repeated over a period of time (although sometimes a single, particularly vicious act counts); plus there's a power difference between the targeted child and the child or children doing the bullying (Menesini and Salmivalli 2017). In other words, the child doing the bullying is older, bigger, tougher, or more socially powerful than the child being bullied. It's the power difference that distinguishes bullying from, say, a heated argument, rudeness, or general thoughtlessness. It's also the power difference that makes it difficult or impossible for children being bullied to protect or defend themselves (Juvonen and Graham 2014).

Bullying is a serious problem. Children who are bullied report lower self-worth and more depressive symptoms, and those symptoms can persist even after the bullying stops (Bogart et al. 2014). Nowadays, the term *bullying* gets thrown around very readily. For example, a young boy I worked with once told me, "I was bullied today!" When I asked what happened, he said, "This kid in my class, he told me, 'Stop making that annoying noise!'" My client didn't have Tourette syndrome, and, while the other boy could certainly have stated his request more politely, this comment doesn't count as bullying.

Unkind behavior that doesn't involve a power difference is not bullying; it's just a conflict or ordinary meanness. In no way does this excuse mean behavior! All of us need to work continuously to make kind choices, to teach children to behave in kind ways, and to promote a kinder world. The distinction between bullying and meanness simply recognizes that there are degrees of severity to peer problems. Calling minor peer difficulties "bullying" can unintentionally tell children, *You're delicate. You can't handle this!* It also trivializes the severe instances of peer abuse.

General Trends in Bullying

Overall rates of many types of bullying and meanness drop steadily from kindergarten to twelfth grade. When children are asked "Does anyone in your class ever hit you? Say mean things to you? Say bad things about you to other kids? Pick on you?" about one in five kindergartners say they experience "a lot" of at least one form of victimization. By sixth grade, only about one in twenty children report this, and by twelfth grade, the rate has dropped to less than one out of a hundred kids (Ladd, Ettekal, and Kochenderfer-Ladd 2017). Social exclusion and other more subtle forms of relational bullying seem to peak in sixth grade, when children are likely to justify rejecting certain peers to support the status and functioning of their own groups (Killen, Mulvey, and Hitti 2013).

Beyond these average trends in bullying, the story can be very different for individual children. Most children are rarely bullied. Others become either more or less victimized over time. A study that followed children from third to sixth grade found that 85.5 percent of children consistently reported that they were rarely victimized, but about 10 percent of children were moderately and increasingly bullied. The remaining 4.5 percent of children started out being frequently bullied but were increasingly less victimized across the three years of the study (Boivin et al. 2010). There can also be overlap between children who bully and their targets. A Dutch study followed ten- to thirteen-year-olds for three years and found that 6 percent of children whom peers identified as victimized turned into bullies, whereas 9 percent of those who bullied turned into victims (Scholte et al. 2007).

Which Kids Are Picked On?

There are two main forms of rejection that make children vulnerable to bullying and other meanness. *Interpersonal rejection* occurs when a particular child's off-putting behavior, such as being aggressive or withdrawn, makes other children dislike him. *Intergroup rejection* happens when a child is a member of a group that peers are biased against. To make things more complicated, sometimes these two types of rejection interact. For example, when children have problem behavior that doesn't fit the stereotype for their gender (such as aggressive girls and withdrawn boys), they tend to have more peer difficulties than kids whose problem behavior is consistent with gender stereotypes (aggressive boys and withdrawn girls) (Kochel et al. 2012). Also, over time, intergroup rejection can bring about interpersonal rejection. For example, a girl who is Muslim in a predominantly Christian school might experience intergroup rejection due to prejudice, which makes her become increasingly withdrawn, leading to interpersonal rejection because peers think she's unfriendly.

Fortunately, encountering meanness from peers isn't necessarily devastating or permanently damaging for children. One encouraging research result comes from a study of cyberbullying in European children. Researchers found that among eleven- to twelve-year-olds who said they had been bullied online, 38 percent said they "got over it straight away," 49 percent said they recovered within a few days, and 11 percent said the effects lasted just a few weeks. Only 2 percent said they were affected for a couple of months or more (Livingstone et al. 2011). Another study found that although 75 percent of middle and high school students believed they had been bullied at some point, only 15 percent said they were noticeably affected by it (Hoover, Oliver, and Hazler 1992). While it's not clear whether the children in these studies were encountering true bullying or more ordinary meanness, it's still good to know that the majority did not believe mistreatment from peers had a lasting effect on them. It's likely that the children who recovered relatively quickly from being the target of peer meanness or bullying had good support at home and good friends at school, so they were better equipped to cope with it. It's also likely that the meanness they encountered was short lived.

But what about those kids who *are* very affected by peer meanness? Ongoing or increasing bullying has more negative effects than bullying that has stopped (Ladd, Ettekal, and Kochenderfer-Ladd 2017). Children who are widely disliked by their peers are especially vulnerable to being targets of meanness. These children believe that being teased is as serious a problem as being the target of threats or physical aggression (Newman and Murray 2005). It may be that widely disliked children are sensitized to even mild forms of aggression because they've been picked on so much or so often. Alternatively, they may have a tendency to overreact to minor incidents, which can put them at risk for further teasing or bullying.

When Your Child Is the Target of Meanness or Bullying

As a parent, when you hear that your child is being treated meanly, it's easy to go into full protective, mother-lioness mode. Obviously, if there's physical danger, you need to step in quickly to ensure safety. This could mean talking to the teacher or the principal, or sending an email to the bus company with a copy to the superintendent. However, keep in mind that your child's version of what happened may not be the full story. For example, your son might say, "He kicked my chair!" and neglect to mention that before the kick, the other boy asked him five times to move his chair over.

Children who are bullied are often reluctant to tell adults because they fear it will make the situation worse. Unfortunately, this is a possibility. One study looked at third through fifth graders who had reported being bullied to a school administrator or parent/guardian. Sadly, one-third of these students said that the school did little or nothing in response. Fewer than one in five said that telling made the bullying stop completely. About one in ten said that the bullying continued or got worse after they reported it (Kevorkian et al. 2016).

We need to be careful not to intervene in ways that could escalate peer problems or to interfere when children could work things out on their own. If there's a way to empower your child to deal with the situation, that's far more helpful than, for example, calling the other parents to tell them what a horrible monster their child is for hurting or upsetting your little lamb. (The other parents are unlikely to respond well to this!)

On the flip side, we don't want to dismiss or minimize children's peer difficulties. It is crushing for children who are being bullied to ask for help from adults and be met with indifference or criticism. Just telling victimized children "You need to be tougher!" or "You should be able to handle this!" isn't helpful, especially when they don't know how to handle it, or when their best efforts haven't improved the situation.

We've all heard stories about a child who was victimized, then gave the bully "one good punch," and that was the end of it! Retaliating is very, very unlikely to stop bullying. First, it doesn't make sense that children who bully will think, *Ah! Now that you've been nasty to me, I'll be kind to you!* Instead, they're likely to fight back harder to assert their dominance. Also, children who bully are adept at targeting kids who are physically, emotionally, or socially weaker than them. Vulnerable children don't need toughening up; they need appropriate guidance and practical support for dealing with very difficult situations.

Anti-Bullying Programs

Bullying and other forms of peer meanness are not easy to solve. Simplistic zero tolerance policies don't work to curb bullying (American Psychological Association Zero Tolerance Task Force 2008). We need thoughtful interventions at many levels. We need to increase awareness among teachers and parents, establish programs that teach children empathy and problem-solving skills, mobilize witnesses to speak up to protect vulnerable children, and create more inclusive schools and communities. Unfortunately, the best-established, whole school antibullying programs only reduce bullying rates about 20 percent (Menesini and Salmivalli 2017). Any decrease in bullying is good, but this is far from good enough. And, if you're the parent of a child who is being victimized, you can't wait for these big-picture solutions to work. You need to deal with the immediate problem of helping your child figure out what to do now.

What We Know About Children's Responses to Bullying

How children respond to meanness or bullying can have a big impact on whether it stops, continues, or even worsens. However, if we look to research for answers about what works in terms of kids responding to bullying or meanness, the answer is a big fat "it depends." Coping strategies have different results depending on the type and severity of victimization, the inclusiveness of the social environment, whether the target is a boy or a girl, and whether the child is rarely or frequently picked on (Visconti and Troop-Gordon 2010).

One thing we do know is that big emotional reactions—either anger or tears—tend to make children more of a target (Kochenderfer-Ladd and Skinner 2002). But beyond that, it's hard to make definite statements about how children who are victimized should respond. Research shows complicated patterns of relationships between coping strategies and victimization. For example, seeking support from peers can be useful, but only if peers respond in warm and helpful ways. Also, for boys, there may be a cost to seeking support, because it may make them look less cool or capable to their peers (Visconti and Troop-Gordon 2010).

Ignoring meanness or bullying is a common response and could make a child seem like a less interesting target, but it could also make the victimized child seem like a passive, easy target or inspire aggressive children to try harder to get a reaction. Ignoring meanness can also make victimized children feel more anxious and lonely.

Problem solving is usually a good way to try to resolve peer difficulties, but victimized children who said that they tried to do this sometimes end up being more rejected. It's possible that their problems were too severe for them to work out on their own. Or, these children may have been clumsy in their efforts, leading peers to think that the victimized children were provoking conflicts rather than trying to solve them. When peers think that children who are victimized do things to cause the meanness they receive, they dislike these vulnerable children and may even conclude that they deserve to be bullied (Graham and Juvonen 2001).

One of the worst things kids can do if they are being picked on is to turn their focus inward and blame themselves for being the target of meanness (Shelley and Craig 2010). No one deserves to be abused. Period.

Real Self-Esteem Tips to Try

Children with low self-esteem tend to internalize meanness from their peers and feel wounded by it. They need to be able to tell themselves, *This is not about me! This is someone who is trying to feel powerful by putting me down. I may not be able to stop it by myself, but I don't have to participate by putting myself down, too.* Although there are no simple answers to what an individual child who is being picked on should do, here are some strategies that might be useful, depending on the situation.

Decide If and How Your Child Should Report the Problem

Kindergartners and first graders usually run to an adult to tell that a peer is being mean. Older kids, on the other hand, need to be more cautious because peers might look down upon them for tattling. If a situation is dangerous or keeps happening, or if there's a power difference that makes it hard for your child to handle the situation alone, it may make sense for your child to report what's happening to the teacher or school counselor. Warn your child not to announce, "I'm telling!" It's better to tell an adult discreetly to minimize peer fallout.

If your child doesn't want to report the problem, and it's not severe enough that you feel you have to report it anyway, there are other options. Simply standing near other kids or an adult at recess time could make your child less of a target for meanness. Another possibility is to alert the teacher and peers to the problem but without tattling. Here's one way to do this: when the aggressive child says something unkind, your child can say in a loud voice, "Quit calling me that!" or "That was a mean thing to say!" then walk away. Most kids don't like to think of themselves as mean, so they won't like the attention they get when your child's remark makes everyone turn around and look at them. Practice this with your child.

Enlist the Teacher's Help

Even if your child doesn't want to report bullying or meanness, you may want to do so. Your child's teacher can be an important resource for understanding what is happening, stepping in to protect your child if needed, and creating a classroom environment in which all children feel safe, accepted, and included. Children are less likely to exclude peers when they believe that their teachers expect them to be kind (Nesdale 2011).

Specific classroom activities can help foster a sense of unity in the classroom. Cooperative games or sharing conversations let students get to know each other and inspire kindness. Well-designed cooperative learning projects, in which children from different ethnic, racial, or ability groups have to work together as equals, generally lead to greater liking and better relationships. In these projects, each child receives part of the necessary information so that all of the children have to teach and learn from each other in order to complete it (Paluck and Green 2009).

Friendly, cooperative, and supportive behaviors from peers—not just the absence of meanness—are important for children's psychological health (Troop-Gordon and Unhjem 2018). Kinder social environments also make it easier for kids to reach out to peers. For example, one study of fifth and sixth graders found that over the course of a school year, anxious withdrawn children who experienced less rejection from their peers were more likely to gradually increase how much they reached out to their peers in positive ways (Gazelle and Rudolph 2004).

Rehearse Responses to Teasing or Rude Questions

Teasing is very common among children, especially boys. That doesn't make it right, but it does mean that knowing how to handle teasing without overreacting is a necessary social skill for children.

Help your child come up with a list of responses to say in a bored tone of voice. The bored tone is crucial. Showing even a shred of anger or upset will encourage the teaser. Your child's comments also shouldn't be mean or stoop to the teaser's level. They just need to express a lack of concern about the teasing. Choose responses that fit your child's age and personality. Here are some possibilities:

"Okay." (Shrug.)

"So what?"

"Thanks for noticing."

"That's so funny I forgot to laugh."

"Really? I never knew that! You're the first person ever to point that out."

"I know what's true, so I won't listen to you."

Use role-play to help your child practice using these. You can say a nonsense word insult, such as "You're a big hurgle murgle!" or "You have gilly mups!" so your child won't feel hurt. Then have your child respond calmly with one of the phrases you've selected together.

Warn your child that there is no response that will instantly make people stop teasing. The goal is just to be boring to prevent the teasing from escalating or spreading to other kids. Eventually, if your child doesn't have a big reaction but also doesn't cower in fear, the teaser is likely to lose interest.

Choose to Ignore Mean Gossip

One sneaky form of bullying involves spreading rumors to attack someone's reputation. This could involve sharing unflattering information or judgments about someone or making up false stories to encourage others to dislike a peer.

Children gossip about each other a lot. For example, Kristina McDonald and her colleagues (2007) video recorded pairs of fourth-grade close girlfriends while they had a short conversation. On average, the girls engaged in thirty-six episodes of gossip, involving twenty-five different people, during the fifteen-minute conversations. Most of the gossip recorded in this study was *not* mean. Over half of the comments just involved sharing information. Another quarter were for entertainment and involved sharing a laugh or an interesting story. Only 7 percent of the gossip comments were aggressive remarks that could hurt someone's social standing.

Gossip can have a positive side. It can help children figure out peer group relationships. Talking about others helps kids understand what behaviors are or are not valued by peers, who is or isn't getting along with whom, and who is or isn't trustworthy. However, mean gossip can also be very hurtful.

Many children fret about what others say about them behind their back. This is not productive, because, whether we like it or not, people are entitled to their private opinions. A more useful attitude is to recognize that what people say about us when we are not present is none of our business. This is extremely difficult for kids to accept. They protest, "But if it's about me, I need to know!" No, they don't.

Nothing good will come of trying to police other people's conversations. Demanding, "Are you talking about me? What did you say about me? What did he say about me?" comes across as self-absorbed and could add fuel to a gossip fire.

Tell your child, "If they don't have the guts to say it to your face, you don't have to deal with it. Besides, the people who know and care about you will continue to know and care about you. Whispered comments won't change that."

You should also warn your child not to repeat any mean comments she hears about others. That just spreads meanness.

Discuss Cyberbullying

Cyberbullying means bullying that occurs through electronic communication. It's far less common than other forms of bullying. In a survey based on a large US sample of over four hundred thousand students in grades three to twelve, about 17 percent of children reported having been verbally bullied whereas only about 4 percent said they'd been cyberbullied. There's also a lot of overlap: 88 percent of kids who have been cyberbullied have been victims of some form of real-life bullying (Olweus 2012).

However, cyberbullying has some characteristics that make it uniquely painful. Cyberbullying is often anonymous or done by people using fake identities, which leaves children wondering who's attacking them and why. It can be very public and easily spread. Also, kids often feel that they can't escape cyberbullying, because it follows them home, even into their bedrooms.

Just like with traditional bullying, combating cyberbullying starts with education. We need to cut through rationalizations and give kids very specific guidance about what kind of behavior is not okay online:

- It's not okay to forward a message sent by someone else. If the sender wants other people to see the message, the sender can pass it along.

- It's not okay to pretend online to be someone you're not. That's not funny; it's deceitful.

- It's not okay to say mean things about someone online, because those comments live forever and spread like cancer.

- It's not okay to post pictures or videos of someone without their consent, especially not ones that would be embarrassing.

- It's not okay to be cruel just because you can't see the face of the person you're hurting.

Spot checks from parents can help ensure that children use electronic communication safely and appropriately.

Warn your child that nothing is private online. A common form of cyberbullying involves setting up someone to say something mean about a classmate and then recording it or forwarding it to that classmate. A variation on this is to prompt the negative comments about a classmate during a video chat and then shift the camera to show that the classmate was right there all along, listening and watching.

To encourage your child to confide in you if he encounters cyber bullying, promise that you won't freak out and cut off access to all electronic communication. Tell your child to take these steps in response to mean messages online:

- Don't answer. Replying will only escalate the battle.

- Take a screenshot. This will be necessary to get help if the cyberbullying is severe or persistent.

- Block the sender or leave a chat that becomes abusive.

- Tell an adult. Online meanness can be painful. No child should have to deal with it alone.

One more tip: collect all phones at sleepovers. This will prevent a lot of difficulties.

Shape the Narrative

As parents, we can't protect our children from having bad things happen to them. It's likely that all children will face meanness from peers in one form or another. For many children, the meanness will be mild, and they will recover quickly. For others, the meanness will be more severe and prolonged.

If your child is the target of bullying, the first step toward recovery is having the bullying end. Often that requires adult intervention. Sometimes it requires moving to a new school or finding extra support from family or other groups.

Once the bullying stops, the next step is to try to shape the narrative of how your child understands what happened. Rather than leave your child with a self-critical and self-defeating story focused on personal flaws and helplessness, try to create a perspective on events that speaks to your child's strength and values and that emphasizes the possibility of growth.

Your narrative might sound something like this:

What those kids did to you was wrong. Nobody deserves to be treated that way. I wish I could have protected you from ever having to go through that. But I'm also proud of you. You could have been nasty back to them, but you weren't. You could have just curled up in a ball and given up, but you didn't. And I bet you'll use this experience somehow. Maybe one day you'll be the one to help someone who's getting picked on. I know you struggled. I know you suffered. But you also kept going and found real friends. It took a lot of inner strength to deal with what you had to deal with. I think it's a pretty great thing to learn about yourself, that even at your age you can face a very difficult situation, and, with the help of people who care about you, get through it.

Wrap-Up

If your child gets bullied or picked on, it can be almost as upsetting for you as it is for your child. There are no simple answers that work for all situations, so you'll need to talk with your child and weigh the options together. Sometimes children with low self-esteem blame themselves for getting bullied. Confront that assumption immediately and forcefully. No one deserves to be treated cruelly, and your child shouldn't participate in the bullying by putting him- or herself down. If your child is in danger or feels frightened, you may need to notify school officials to keep your child safe even if your child doesn't want you to do so. On the other hand, if the meanness is milder and doesn't involve a power difference, you may want to coach your child on some ways to respond.

Up to now, this book has addressed the wide varieties of difficulties associated with low self-esteem, from problems with relationships to problems persevering with hard work or being overly perfectionistic to problems with making decisions, gaining a sense of belonging, or dealing with meanness from peers. We've emphasized that lowering self-focus can help children move forward in positive ways. The final chapter in this book looks at the positive experiences that occur when children are able to mute self-judgment and self-criticism and move toward a quiet ego.

Take-Home Points

- Meanness is common among children.

- If unkind behavior doesn't involve a power difference, then it's not bullying.

- Ongoing or increasing bullying has more negative effects on children than bullying that has stopped.

- Ending bullying often requires adult intervention.

Real Self-Esteem and the Joys of a Quiet Ego

One time, a middle-school girl I worked with finally worked up the courage to tell me her deepest fear. Her body was so tense, it was practically vibrating, as she gasped out, "What if I grow up to be ordinary?" This fear is one that I see often, especially in bright, capable kids, and I think it speaks to a deep problem: fragile self-esteem built on a shaky base of self-focus and self-promotion.

The parents of pretty much every client in my practice tell me at some point, "My child has low self-esteem." To the outside world, these children might or might not appear confident. But their parents see these children's late-night tears related to feeling overwhelmed by schoolwork, endless fretting about what they said or did that someone might have thought was weird, frantic avoidance of any situation where they might not look perfect, and vicious self-criticism when they make a mistake. What I think the parents are picking up on is the vulnerability of their children's self-worth. One mistake, one small criticism, one tiny slight, and these kids crash, feeling hopelessly flawed.

Then vs. Now

From a modern perspective, the 1990s focus on giving trophies to everyone and having children chant, "I'm special!" seems silly.

Obviously, empty praise can't help children develop genuine confidence. But nowadays, children are growing up with a cultural focus on *seeking applause*, which I believe is far more dangerous to their well-being. Like the girl I mentioned at the start of this chapter, many of the children and teens I see in my practice think there are only two options in life: to be impressive or to be worthless.

Stories about rising rates of anxiety and depression in teens abound in the media, but I'm hearing increasing concerns about self-image from even young children: the sixth grader who feels rejected when no one likes the selfie she posts online; the fifth grader who is convinced he has no friends because his sneakers aren't cool enough; the fourth grader who just made the baseball team but feels dejected because he isn't starting; the third grader who is in tears because she thinks doing badly on a spelling test means she'll never get into a good college; the second grader who cries and says, "I'm the worst kid in the world!" when his parents scold him for squabbling with his sister; the first grader who feels ashamed because she's heavier than her classmates. All of these children are judging themselves and believing they are flawed.

Cultural messages about having to be great and look good put enormous pressure on children who buy into them. When kids inevitably fall short of being amazing at all times, they can feel crushed. Some children respond by anxiously pushing themselves harder to prove their worth. Some give up in helpless dejection. And some don't even try—they're too afraid of looking bad or being embarrassed to attempt anything that they can't instantly do well.

Another, More Holistic Approach to Self-Esteem

The problem for children with low self-esteem isn't so much that they think they're inadequate; the problem is that they're trapped by their unrelenting self-criticism. It's their preoccupation with judging themselves that makes them miserable and gets in the way of their relationships and achievement. Fixating on promoting, protecting, defending, or evaluating the self is often a painful distraction that hinders contentment and healthy relationships (Leary 2007).

This book is loaded with ideas of ways to help children who struggle with low self-esteem, but none of these strategies involve trying to *increase* children's self-esteem or convince them that they're amazing. In fact, the approach described in this book has nothing to do with old ideas of trying to boost self-esteem. Instead, we looked at ways to ease critical self-focus by helping children meet their fundamental needs for connection, competence, and choice (Ryan and Deci 2000).

The chapters on connection focused on helping children build healthy relationships with their parents, siblings, and peers. These relationships give children a base of support that steadies them and pulls them out of negative self-focus.

The chapters on competence looked at ways to help children embrace learning so that they see their current level of performance as a momentary event rather than a permanent verdict on their ability and worth as a human being. Knowing that they can continue to grow and learn and become more capable frees children to sustain effort without either giving up or beating themselves up for mistakes.

The chapters on choice talked about ways to help children with low self-esteem find their voice, empowering them to make decisions about what matters to them. We also discussed ways to help children evaluate cultural messages about how they ought to look and act and to seek out groups where they can find a genuine sense of community.

When children are able to meet their needs for connection, competence, and choice, they are better equipped to move past their preoccupation with trying to evaluate or prove their worth. It's not that they suddenly start to believe that they're wonderful. With real self-esteem, they're too busy living to get stuck on judging themselves.

The bulk of this book focused on addressing problems that get in the way of children developing real self-esteem. We talked about specific ways to help children ease away from critical self-judgments that keep kids stuck. But beyond the goal of reducing unrelenting self-focus, what does real self-esteem look like? What are we aiming for?

The Quiet Ego and Real Self-Esteem

In psychology, there's been a growing interest in the idea of a *quiet ego* (Leary and Diebels 2013; Wayment and Bauer 2008). Heidi Wayment and her colleagues (2015) define a quiet ego as a state in which "the volume of the ego is turned down so that it might listen to others as well as the self in an effort to approach life more humanely and compassionately." Having a quiet ego is a way of being in the world that is not preoccupied with self-judgment and instead embraces a compassionate view of self and others that allows for both present awareness and growth. A quiet ego is the ultimate expression of real self-esteem.

In many ways, the notion of a quiet ego is a rediscovery of an old idea. The ideal of moving beyond self-absorption is part of most religions and philosophical traditions and goes back at least three thousand years in Buddhism. Having a quiet ego doesn't involve putting oneself down (which is a form of self-focus). It's a kind of forgetting of the self through recognizing that we are just a tiny piece of the larger universe and definitely not the center of it!

Various threads of research have given us a picture of what adults who tend to have quiet egos are like (Leary et al. 2017). They are usually calm and confident without necessarily drawing attention to themselves. They focus on the present rather than worry about the future or regret the past. They're less likely to get ruffled by negative events, because they don't take them personally or spend time and energy wondering *Why me?* They're not defensive about mistakes, and they're not overly concerned about their public image.

They're good at thinking in terms of *we* rather than *I*. In their interactions with others, they're generally agreeable and caring.

Most of us adults fall far short of the pure, transcendent enlightenment of a quiet ego in our daily lives. So how can we expect children, especially those with low self-esteem, to do all of this? The abilities that underlie the development of a quiet ego include perspective taking, empathy, moral judgment, and identification with broader groups (Bauer 2008). These are skills that children develop only gradually, but they are absolutely worth cultivating and supporting.

Susan Harter (2017), who has studied children's self-esteem extensively, says that there's very little evidence of quiet ego states in children. I disagree. Although children can certainly be self-absorbed, in some ways, they are better than adults at having a quiet ego. Think of the last time you saw your child curiously exploring, engrossed in a project, or belly laughing with a friend. These are common but precious moments of freedom from self-consciousness.

For most of us, a quiet ego is aspirational, not something we can maintain at all times. Fortunately, there are experiences of quiet ego states that are accessible to everyone, including children. These experiences may be fleeting, but they give us glimpses of what is possible when we're able to move past self-focus (Leary and Guadagno 2011). Below are some examples. We can't do all of them all of the time, but occasionally experiencing one or more of these quiet ego states is inspiring.

Mindfulness

Mindfulness involves deliberately focusing on the present moment in a nonjudgmental way (e.g., Kabat-Zinn 1994). It can be part of a meditation practice or simply a moment of awareness. Practicing mindfulness can be very useful in quieting noisy self-focus.

Several studies have found that school-based mindfulness meditation interventions with children as young as preschool can decrease stress and aggression and improve cognitive performance (Flook et al. 2015; Schonert-Reichl et al. 2015; Zenner, Herrnleben-Kurz, and Walach 2014).

Can young children really do mindfulness? Probably not in the same way that adults can. However, they can begin to focus their attention, for a moment or a few minutes, and just observe what is happening in them and around them. Even four-year-olds can be invited to focus on their breathing or watch glitter settle in a jar of water. Five- to eight-year-olds are increasingly aware of the ongoing flow of their thoughts (Pillow 2012). They could learn, for example, to focus on a sound, listening until it fades, or to do a scan of their body, just noticing what they experience, and bringing their attention back when it wanders. Older children could be guided to notice their thoughts without necessarily believing them, judging them, or trying to change them. Children can also practice concentrating on thoughts of loving-kindness.

Mindfulness works best if it's a regular practice. An app can be a good way to introduce meditation to your child. Choose one that's specifically designed for kids and do it together.

Flow

Mihaly Csikszentmihalyi (2008) coined the term *flow* to refer to a state in which we are so absorbed in doing a task that we are utterly unselfconscious and lose track of time. We are completely immersed in the process rather than fretting about the outcome. Flow is most likely to occur when the challenge of a task matches our ability. If the task is too hard, we feel anxious; if it's too easy, we're bored. Flow is an engrossing focus on *now* that feels deeply satisfying, intensely enjoyable, and personally meaningful.

The more flow we have in our lives, the happier we are. You may have seen your child immersed in a flow state while building with Legos, drawing, reading, swimming, shooting baskets, or even digging in a sandbox. Describe the idea of flow; then ask your child what activities bring on that delicious quiet ego state.

Compassion

An integral part of a quiet ego is the ability to think beyond ourselves. *Compassion* is a feeling of concern for others' suffering that motivates a desire to help (Goetz, Keltner, and Simon-Thomas 2010). Although there can be benefits to the self from helping others, compassion is mainly oriented outward, away from the self and toward the person who is hurt. Personal distress gets in the way of compassion. If children are too upset, they'll be motivated to help themselves by running away from a situation rather than moving toward it to help someone else (Eisenberg et al. 1989).

Children learn compassion partly through receiving it from parents. Caring about a friend can prompt children to respond with concern when that friend is hurt or upset. Volunteer work in the broader community can be another way for kids to learn compassion.

Elevation

Elevation is the word Jonathan Haidt (2000) uses to describe the feeling we get when witnessing "acts of moral beauty or virtue" (1). For example, after seeing an inspiring news clip about an altruistic hero, we might feel strongly moved and uplifted. Elevation involves experiencing a warm opening sensation in our chest, as if our heart were expanding, and an increased motivation to help others. Elevation pulls us out of ourselves and makes us feel optimistic about the human race. It also motivates us to care for others (Schnall, Roper, and Fessler 2010) and can even inspire spirituality (Van Cappellen et al. 2013).

Although the research on elevation involves college students and adults, it also seems relevant for kids who are eight- or nine-years-old or older. Heartwarming novels and movies could allow children to experience the delight of elevation.

Awe

Finally, another common quiet ego state is awe. Awe is a feeling of wonder and amazement that comes when we encounter extraordinary beauty or greatness that transcends our current understanding. It can be triggered by a vast panoramic view of nature, an exquisite piece of music or art, or a profoundly moving religious experience. Awe makes us feel small and pleasantly insignificant but also connected to something bigger than ourselves. It directs our attention away from the self and toward our environment in an expansive way. It inspires generosity and helpfulness (Piff et al. 2015).

Again, the research on awe involves adults, but this feeling seems very accessible to children in late elementary school and older. Visiting the beach, going on a hike, or just gazing at the stars with your child can set the stage for awe.

The Real Self-Esteem Revolution, Getting Past Self-Focus

Children today face unprecedented pressure to perform. From high-stakes testing to nonstop social media to highly competitive sports and extracurricular activities, every inch of their lives seems to be subject to judgment. Add in the global competition, growing economic inequality, and job insecurity that their parents experience, and it's a recipe for self-doubt.

I believe all of these factors have led many children to develop an anxious preoccupation with their worth. When self-judgment consumes their awareness, they focus excessively on trying to look good or worry that they don't measure up. They fear criticism and failure, so they avoid, hide, or defend mistakes or become paralyzed by a sense of painful inadequacy.

What we need, as a culture, is a revolution in how we understand self-esteem. Instead of trying to promote high self-esteem, we need to find ways to move past self-focus. When children are less concerned with evaluating, comparing, protecting, defending, promoting, or enhancing their self-image, they're freer to empathize with others, genuinely engage in learning, and identify with values that are bigger than themselves.

The pinch of rejection or failure or uncertainty can so easily pull us into a self-critical mode. But we can recognize when we're there and learn to be gentler with ourselves. We can recognize the trap of self-judgment and seek out experiences that cultivate a quiet ego. And we can guide our children toward this healthier alternative to running on the constant treadmill of trying to prove their worth.

Our children don't have to work on loving themselves. They need to move past self-focus toward a quiet ego. Real self-esteem is about being able to let go of the question *Am I good enough?* in order to create a fuller, richer life.

Works Cited and Consulted

Abuhatoum, S., and N. Howe. 2013. "Power in Sibling Conflict During Early and Middle Childhood." *Social Development* 22 (4): 738–54.

Adler, P. A., and P. Adler. 1995. "Dynamics of Inclusion and Exclusion in Preadolescent Cliques." *Social Psychology Quarterly* 58 (3): 145–62.

Alberts, A., D. Elkind, and S. Ginsberg. 2007. "The Personal Fable and Risk-Taking in Early Adolescence." *Journal of Youth and Adolescence* 36 (1): 71–76.

Algoe, S. B., and J. Haidt. 2009. "Witnessing Excellence in Action: The 'Other-Praising' Emotions of Elevation, Gratitude, and Admiration." *The Journal of Positive Psychology* 4 (2): 105–27.

American Psychological Association Zero Tolerance Task Force. 2008. "Are Zero Tolerance Policies Effective in the Schools?: An Evidentiary Review and Recommendations." *The American Psychologist* 63 (9): 852–62.

Arnett, J. J., K. H. Trzesniewski, and M. B. Donnellan. 2013. "The Dangers of Generational Myth-Making: Rejoinder to Twenge." *Emerging Adulthood* 1 (1): 17–20.

Bagwell, C. L., J. D. Coie, R. A. Terry, and J. E. Lochman. 2000. "Peer Clique Participation and Social Status in Preadolescence." *Merrill–Palmer Quarterly* 46 (2): 280–305.

Bai, S., R. L. Repetti, and J. B. Sperling. 2016. "Children's Expressions of Positive Emotion Are Sustained by Smiling, Touching, and Playing with Parents and Siblings: A Naturalistic Observational Study of Family Life." *Developmental Psychology* 52 (1): 88–101.

Bandura, A. 1962. "Social Learning Through Imitation." In *Nebraska Symposium on Motivation*, edited by M. R. Jones, Lincoln, NE: University of Nebraska Press.

———. 2008. "An Agentic Perspective on Positive Psychology." In *Discovering Human Strengths*. Positive Psychology: Exploring the Best in People, vol. 1, edited by S. J. Lopez. Westport, CT: Praeger Publishers/Greenwood Publishing Group.

Bank, S. P., and M. D. Kahn. 2003. *The Sibling Bond*, anniversary ed. New York: Basic Books.

Baron, A. S., and M. R. Banaji. 2006. "The Development of Implicit Attitudes: Evidence of Race Evaluations from Ages 6 and 10 and Adulthood." *Psychological Science*, 17 (1): 53–58.

Bauer, J. J. 2008. "How the Ego Quiets As It Grows: Ego Development, Growth Stories, and Eudaimonic Personality Development." In *Transcending Self-Interest: Psychological Explorations of the Quiet Ego*, edited by H. A. Wayment and J. J. Bauer. Washington, DC: American Psychological Association.

Baumeister, R. F., J. D. Campbell, J. I. Krueger, and K. D. Vohs. 2003. "Does High Self-Esteem Cause Better Performance, Interpersonal Success, Happiness, or Healthier Lifestyles?" *Psychological Science in the Public Interest* 4 (1): 1–44.

Bell, J. H., and R. D. Bromnick. 2003. "The Social Reality of the Imaginary Audience: A Grounded Theory Approach." *Adolescence* 38 (150): 205–19.

Berger, C., and P. C. Rodkin. 2012. "Group Influences on Individual Aggression and Prosociality: Early Adolescents Who Change Peer Affiliations." *Social Development* 21 (2): 396–413.

Bigler, R. S., C. S. Brown, and M. Markell. 2001. "When Groups Are Not Created Equal: Effects of Group Status on the Formation of Intergroup Attitudes in Children." *Child Development* 72 (4): 1151–62.

Blatt, S. J. 1974. "Levels of Object Representation in Anaclitic and Introjective Depression." *Psychoanalytic Study of the Child*, 29: 107–57.

———. 2004. *Experiences of Depression: Theoretical Clinical, and Research Perspectives*. Washington, DC: American Psychological Association.

Bleske-Rechek, A., and J. Kelley. 2014. "Birth Order and Personality: A Within-Family Test Using Independent Self-Reports from Both Firstborn and Laterborn Siblings." *Personality and Individual Differences*, 56: 15–18.

Bogart, L. M., M. N. Elliott, D. J. Klein, S. R. Tortolero, S. Mrug, M. F. Peskin, S. L. Davies, E. T. Schink, and M. A. Schuster. 2014. "Peer Victimization in Fifth Grade and Health in Tenth Grade." *Pediatrics* 133 (3): 440–47.

Boivin, M., A. Petitclerc, B. Feng, and E. D. Barker. 2010. "The Developmental Trajectories of Peer Victimization in Middle to Late Childhood and the Changing Nature of Their Behavioral Correlates." *Merrill-Palmer Quarterly*, 56 (3): 231–60.

Brown, B. 2015. *Daring Greatly: How the Courage to Be Vulnerable Transforms the Way We Live, Love, Parent, and Lead*. Rep. ed. New York: Penguin.

Brown, B. B., and E. L. Dietz. 2009. "Informal Peer Groups in Middle Childhood and Adolescence." In *Handbook of Peer Interactions, Relationships, and Groups*, edited by K. H. Rubin, W. M. Bukowski, and B. Laursen. New York: Guilford Press.

Brown, K. W., and M. R. Leary. 2017. *The Oxford Handbook of Hypo-Egoic Phenomena*. New York: Oxford University Press.

Brummelman, E., J. Crocker, and B. J. Bushman. 2016. "The Praise Paradox: When and Why Praise Backfires in Children with Low Self-Esteem." *Child Development Perspectives* 10 (2): 111–15.

Brummelman, E., S. Thomaes, B. Orobio de Castro, G. Overbeek, and B. J. Bushman. 2014a. "That's Not Just Beautiful—That's Incredibly Beautiful!: The Adverse Impact of Inflated Praise on Children with Low Self-Esteem." *Psychological Science* 25 (3): 728–35.

Brummelman, E., S. Thomaes, G. Overbeek, B. Orobio de Castro, M. A. van den Hout, and B. J. Bushman. 2014b. "On Feeding Those Hungry for Praise: Person Praise Backfires in Children with Low Self-Esteem." *Journal of Experimental Psychology: General* 143 (1): 9–14.

Buhrmester, D. 1992. "The Developmental Courses of Sibling and Peer Relationships." In *Children's Sibling Relationships: Developmental and Clinical Issues*, edited by F. Boer and J. Dunn. Hillsdale, NJ: Erlbaum.

Bukowksi, W. J., C. Motzoi, and F. Meyer. 2009. "Friendship As Process, Function, and Outcome." In *Handbook of Peer Interactions, Relationships, and Groups*, edited by K. H. Rubin, W. M. Bukowski, and B. Laursen. New York: Guilford Press.

Callahan, D. 2013. "Obesity: Chasing an Elusive Epidemic." *The Hastings Center Report* 43 (1): 34–40.

Campos, B., A. P. Graesch, R. Repetti, T. Bradbury, and E. Ochs. 2009. "Opportunity for Interaction? A Naturalistic Observation Study of Dual-Earner Families After Work and School." *Journal of Family Psychology* 23 (6): 798–807.

Chang, R. 2017. "Hard Choices." *Journal of the American Philosophical Association* 3 (1): 1–21.

Cillessen, A. H. N., and L. Mayeux. 2004a. "From Censure to Reinforcement: Developmental Changes in the Association Between Aggression and Social Status." *Child development* 75 (1): 147–63.

———. 2004b. "Sociometric Status and Peer Group Behavior: Previous Findings and Current Directions." In *Children's Peer Relations: From Development to Intervention*, edited by J. B. Kupersmidt and K. A. Dodge. Washington, DC: American Psychological Association.

Common Sense Media. 2015. "Children, Teens, Media, and Body Image: A Common Sense Media Research Brief." January 21. https://www

.commonsensemedia.org/research/children-teens-media-and
-body-image.

Cooley, C. H. (1902) 1983. *Human Nature and the Social Order.* New York: Charles Scribner's Sons. Reprint, New Brunswick, NJ: Transaction. Citation refers to the reprint edition.

Credé, M., M. C. Tynan, and P. D. Harms. 2017. "Much Ado About Grit: A Meta-Analytic Synthesis of the Grit Literature." *Journal of Personality and Social Psychology* 113 (3): 492–511.

Crocker, J., S. Moeller, and A. Burson. 2010. "The Costly Pursuit of Self-Esteem: Implications for Self-Regulation." In *Handbook of Personality and Self-Regulation,* edited by R. H. Hoyle. Chichester, UK: Wiley.

Crocker, J., and L. E. Park. 2004. The Costly Pursuit of Self-Esteem. *Psychological Bulletin* 130 (3): 392–414.

Crockett, L., M. Losoff, and A. C. Petersen. 1984. "Perceptions of the Peer Group and Friendship in Early Adolescence." *The Journal of Early Adolescence* 4 (2): 155–81.

Csikszentmihalyi, M. 2008. *Flow: The Psychology of Optimal Experience.* New York: Harper Perennial Modern Classics.

Cvencek, D., A. G. Greenwald, and A. N. Meltzoff. 2016. "Implicit Measures for Preschool Children Confirm Self-Esteem's Role in Maintaining a Balanced Identity." *Journal of Experimental Social Psychology* 62: 50–57.

Damian, R. I., and B. W. Roberts. 2015. "Settling the Debate on Birth Order and Personality." *Proceedings of the National Academy of Sciences of the United States of America* 112 (46): 14119–20.

Damian, L. E., J. Stoeber, O. Negru-Subtirica, and A. Baban. 2017. "On the Development of Perfectionism: The Longitudinal Role of Academic Achievement and Academic Efficacy." *Journal of Personality* 85 (4): 565–77.

Damon, W. 1995. *Greater Expectations: Overcoming the Culture of Indulgence in America's Homes and Schools.* Old Tappan, NJ: The Free Press.

Davies, D. 2011. *Child Development: A Practitioner's Guide,* 3rd ed. New York: Guilford Press.

Davis, E. L., L. J. Levine, H. C. Lench, and J. A. Quas. 2010. "Metacognitive Emotion Regulation: Children's Awareness That Changing Thoughts and Goals Can Alleviate Negative Emotions." *Emotion* 10: 498–510.

Dodge, K. A., D. G. Schlundt, I. Schocken, and J. D. Delugach. 1983. "Social Competence and Children's Sociometric Status: The Role of Peer Group Entry Strategies." *Merrill-Palmer Quarterly* 29 (3): 309–36.

Duckworth, A. 2016. *Grit: The Power of Passion and Perseverance.* New York: Scribner.

Duckworth, A. L., C. Peterson, M. D. Matthews, and D. R. Kelly. 2007. "Grit: Perseverance and Passion for Long-Term Goals." *Journal of Personality and Social Psychology* 92 (6): 1087–101.

Dunlosky, J., K. A. Rawson, E. J. Marsh, M. J. Nathan, and D. T. Willingham. 2013. "Improving Students' Learning with Effective Learning Techniques: Promising Directions from Cognitive and Educational Psychology." *Psychological Science in the Public Interest* 14 (1): 4–58.

Dunn, J., and C. Kendrick. 1982. *Siblings: Love, Envy, and Understanding.* Cambridge, MA: Harvard University Press.

Dunn, J., and P. Munn, P. 1985. "Becoming a Family Member: Family Conflict and the Development of Social Understanding in the Second Year." *Child Development* 56 (2): 480–92.

Dweck, C. S. 2006. *Mindset: The New Psychology of Success.* New York: Random House.

Eisenberg, N., R. A. Fabes, P. A. Miller, J. Fultz, R. Shell, R. M. Mathy, and R. R. Reno. 1989. "Relation of Sympathy and Personal Distress to Prosocial Behavior: A Multimethod Study." *Journal of Personality and Social Psychology* 57 (1): 55–66.

Elkind, D. 1967. "Egocentrism in Adolescence." *Child Development* 38 (4): 1025–34.

Ellis, W. E., and L. Zarbatany. 2017. "Understanding Processes of Peer Clique Influence in Late Childhood and Early Adolescence." *Child Development Perspectives* 11 (4): 227–32.

Eskreis-Winkler L., A. L. Duckworth, E. Shulman, and S. Beale S. 2014. "The Grit Effect: Predicting Retention in the Military, the Workplace, School and Marriage." *Frontiers in Psychology* 5: 36.

Eyberg, S. M. 1988. "Parent-Child Interaction Therapy: Integration of Traditional and Behavioral Concerns." *Child and Family Behavior Therapy* 10 (1): 33–46.

Falconer, C. W., K. G. Wilson, and J. Falconer. 1990. "A Psychometric Investigation of Gender-Tilted Families: Implications for Family Therapy." *Family Relations* 39 (1): 8–13.

Field, T. 2010. "Touch for Socioemotional and Physical Well-Being: A Review." *Developmental Review* 30 (4): 367–83.

Flook, L., S. B. Goldberg, L. Pinger, and R. J. Davidson. 2015. "Promoting Prosocial Behavior and Self-Regulatory Skills in Preschool Children Through a Mindfulness-Based Kindness Curriculum." *Developmental Psychology* 51 (1): 44–51.

Frankenberger, K. 2000. "Adolescent Egocentrism: A Comparison Among Adolescents and Adults." *Journal of Adolescence* 23 (3): 343–54.

Furukawa, E., J. Tangney, and F. Higashibara. 2012. "Cross-Cultural Continuities and Discontinuities in Shame, Guilt, and Pride: A Study of Children Residing in Japan, Korea, and the USA." *Self and Identity* 11 (1): 90–113.

Galanaki, E. P. 2012. "The Imaginary Audience and the Personal Fable: A Test of Elkind's Theory of Adolescent Egocentrism." *Psychology* 3 (6): 457–66.

Gazelle, H. 2010. "Anxious Solitude/Withdrawal And Anxiety Disorders: Conceptualization, Co-Occurrence, and Peer Processes Leading Toward and Away from Disorder in Childhood." In *Social Anxiety in Childhood: Bridging Developmental and Clinical Perspectives*, edited by H. Gazelle and K. H. Rubin, *New Directions for Child and Adolescent Development* 127: 67–78. San Francisco: Jossey-Bass.

Gazelle, H., and K. D. Rudolph. 2004. "Moving Toward and Away from the World: Social Approach and Avoidance Trajectories in Anxious Solitary Youth." *Child Development* 75 (3): 829–49.

Germer, C. K., and K. D. Neff. 2013. "Self-Compassion in Clinical Practice." *Journal of Clinical Psychology* 69 (8): 856–67.

Gest, S. D., S.A. Graham-Bermann, and W. W. Hartup. 2001. "Peer experience: Common and Unique Features of Number of Friendships, Social Network Centrality, and Sociometric Status." *Social Development* 10 (1): 23–40.

Gifford-Smith, M. E., and C. A. Brownell. 2003. "Childhood Peer Relationships: Social Acceptance, Friendships, and Peer Networks." *Journal of School Psychology* 41 (4): 235–84.

Gilbert, D. 2006. *Stumbling on Happiness*. New York: Knopf.

Gilbert, P., and S. Procter. 2006. "Compassionate Mind Training for People with High Shame and Self-Criticism: Overview and Pilot Study of a Group Therapy Approach." *Clinical Psychology and Psychotherapy* 13: 353–79.

Goetz, J. L., D. Keltner, and E. Simon-Thomas. 2010. "Compassion: An Evolutionary Analysis and Empirical Review." *Psychological Bulletin* 136 (3): 351–74.

Graham, S., and J. Juvonen. 2001. "An Attributional Approach to Peer Victimization." In *Peer Harassment in School: The Plight of the Vulnerable and Victimized*, edited by J. Juvonen and S. Graham. New York: Guilford Press.

Greene, R. 2016. *Raising Human Beings: Creating a Collaborative Partnership with Your Child*. New York: Scribner.

Haidt, J. 2000. "The Positive Emotion of Elevation." *Prevention and Treatment* 3 (1): article 3c.

Haimovitz, K., and C. S. Dweck. 2017. "The Origins of Children's Growth and Fixed Mindsets: New Research and a New Proposal." *Child Development* 88 (6): 1849–59.

Hart, D., R. Atkins, and N. Tursi. 2006. "Origins and Developmental Influences on Self-Esteem." In *Self-Esteem Issues and Answers*, edited by M. H. Kernis. London: Psychology Press.

Harter, S. 1990. "Developmental Differences in the Nature of Self-Representations: Implications for the Understanding, Assessment, and Treatment of Maladaptive Behavior." *Cognitive Therapy and Research* 14 (2): 113–42.

———. 2000. "Is Self-Esteem Only Skin-Deep? The Inextricable Link Between Physical Appearance and Self-Esteem." *Reclaiming Children and Youth* 9 (3): 133–38.

———. 2006. "The Self." In *Social, Emotional, and Personality Development*. Handbook of Child Psychology, vol. 3., edited by N. Eisenberg, W. Damon and R. Lerner. 6th ed. New York: John Wiley and Sons.

———. 2012. "Emerging Self Processes During Childhood and Adolescence." In *Handbook of Self and Identity*, edited by M. Leary and J. Tangney. 2nd ed. New York: Guilford Press.

———. 2015. *The Construction of the Self: Developmental and Sociocultural Foundations*, 2nd ed. New York: Guilford Press.

———. 2017. "Developmental and Prosocial Dimensions of Hypo-egoic Phenomena." In *The Oxford Handbook of Hypo-egoic Phenomena*, edited by K. W. Brown and M. R. Leary. New York: Oxford University Press.

Hembree-Kigin, T. L., and C. B. McNeil. 1995. *Parent-Child Interaction Therapy*. New York: Plenum Press.

Henderlong, J., and M. R. Lepper. 2002. "The Effects of Praise on Children's Intrinsic Motivation: A Review and Synthesis." *Psychological Bulletin* 128 (5): 774–95.

Herschell, A. D., E. J. Calzada, S. M. Eyberg, and C. B. McNeil. 2002. "Clinical Issues in Parent-Child Interaction Therapy." *Cognitive and Behavioral Practice* 9 (1): 16–27.

Hetherington, E. M. 1988. "Parents, Children and Siblings: Six Years After Divorce." In *Relationships Within Families: Mutual Influences*, edited by R. A. Hinde and J. Stevenson-Hinde. Oxford: Oxford University Press.

Hoover, J. H., R. Oliver, and R. J. Hazler. 1992. "Bullying: Perceptions of Adolescent Victims in the Midwestern USA." *School Psychology International* 13 (1): 5–16.

Howe, N., C. Rinaldi, M. Jennings, and H. Petrakos. 2002. "No! The Lambs Can Stay Out Because They Got Cosies: Constructive and Destructive Sibling Conflict, Pretend Play, and Social Understanding." *Child Development* 73 (5): 1460–73.

Howe, N., H. S. Ross, and H. Recchia. 2011. "Sibling Relations in Early and Middle Childhood." In *The Wiley-Blackwell Handbook of Childhood Social Development*, edited by P. K. Smith and C. Hart. Malden, MA: Blackwell Publishing.

Hughes, D., J. Rodriguez, E. P. Smith, D. J. Johnson, H. C. Stevenson, and P. Spicer. 2006. "Parents' Ethnic-Racial Socialization Practices: A Review of Research and Directions for Future Study." *Developmental Psychology* 42 (4): 747–70.

Iyengar, S. S., and M. R. Lepper. 2000. "When Choice Is Demotivating: Can One Desire Too Much of a Good Thing?" *Journal of Personality and Social Psychology* 79 (6): 995–1006.

Juvonen, J., and S. Graham. 2014. "Bullying in Schools: The Power of Bullies and the Plight of Victims." *Annual Review of Psychology* 65 (1): 159–85.

Kabat-Zinn, J. 1994. *Wherever You Go, There You Are: Mindfulness Meditation in Everyday Life*. New York: Hachette Books.

Kasser, T. 2002. *The High Price of Materialism*. Cambridge, MA: MIT Press.

———. 2005. "Frugality, Generosity, and Materialism in Children and Adolescents." In *What Do Children Need to Flourish?*, edited by K. A. Moore, and L. H. Lippman. New York: Springer.

Kevorkian, M. M., A. Rodriguez, M. P. Earnhardt, T. D. Kennedy, R. D'Antona, A. G. Russom, and J. Borror. 2016. "Bullying in Elementary Schools." *Journal of Child and Adolescent Trauma* 9 (4): 267–76.

Killen, M., K. L. Mulvey, and A. Hitti. 2013. "Social Exclusion in Childhood: A Developmental Intergroup Perspective." *Child Development* 84 (2): 772–90.

Kim, J., S. McHale, D. Osgood, and A. Crouter. 2006. "Longitudinal Course and Family Correlates of Sibling Relationships from Childhood Through Adolescence." *Child Development* 77 (6): 1746–61.

Kochel, K. P., C. F. Miller, K. A. Updegraff, G. W. Ladd, and B. Kochenderfer-Ladd. 2012. "Associations Between Fifth Graders' Gender Atypical Problem Behavior and Peer Relationships: A Short-Term Longitudinal Study." *Journal of Youth and Adolescence* 41 (8): 1022–34.

Kochenderfer-Ladd, B., and K. Skinner. 2002. "Children's Coping Strategies: Moderators of the Effects of Peer Victimization." *Developmental Psychology* 38 (2): 267–78.

Kopala-Sibley, D. C., D. C. Zuroff, B. L. Hankin, and J. R. Abela. 2015. "The Development of Self-Criticism and Dependency in Early Adolescence and Their Role in the Development of Depressive and Anxiety Symptoms." *Personality and Social Psychology Bulletin* 41 (8): 1094–109.

Kopala-Sibley, D. C., D. C. Zuroff, M. J. Leybman, and N. Hope. 2013. "Recalled Peer Relationship Experiences and Current Levels of Self-Criticism and Self-Reassurance." *Psychology and Psychotherapy: Theory, Research, and Practice* 86: 33–51.

Kowal, A. K., J. L. Krull, and L. Kramer. 2006. "Shared Understanding of Parental Differential Treatment in Families." *Social Development* 15 (2): 276–95.

Kramer, L. 2010. "The Essential Ingredients of Successful Sibling Relationships: An Emerging Framework for Advancing Theory and Practice." *Child Development Perspectives* 4 (2): 80–86.

Kramer, L., L. A. Perozynski, and T. Y. Chung. 1999. "Parental Responses to Sibling Conflict: The Effects of Development and Parent Gender." *Child Development* 70 (6): 1401–14.

Kross, E., and O. Ayduk. 2017. "Self-Distancing: Theory, Research, and Current Directions." *Advances in Experimental Social Psychology* 55: 81–136.

Kross, E., M. G. Berman, W. Mischel, E. E. Smith, and T. D. Wager. 2011a. "Social Rejection Shares Somatosensory Representations with Physical Pain." *Proceedings of the National Academy of Sciences* 108 (15): 6270–75.

Kross, E., A. Duckworth, O. Ayduk, E. Tsukayama, and W. Mischel. 2011b. "The Effect of Self-Distancing on Adaptive Versus Maladaptive Self-Reflection in Children." *Emotion* 11 (5): 1032–39.

Kuster, F., U. Orth, and L. L. Meier. 2012. "Rumination Mediates the Prospective Effect of Low Self-Esteem on Depression: A Five-Wave Longitudinal Study." *Personality and Social Psychology Bulletin* 38 (6): 747–59.

Kwon, K., A. M. Lease, and L. Hoffman. 2012. "The Impact of Clique Membership on Children's Social Behavior and Status Nominations." *Social Development* 21 (1): 150–169.

Ladd, G. W., I. Ettekal, and B. Kochenderfer-Ladd. 2017. "Peer Victimization Trajectories from Kindergarten Through High School:

Differential Pathways for Children's School Engagement and Achievement?" *Journal of Educational Psychology* 109 (6): 826–41.

Lapsley, D. K., and M. Murphy. 1985. "Another Look at the Theoretical Assumptions of Adolescent Egocentrism." *Developmental Review* 5 (3): 201–17.

Leary, M. R. 2007. *The Curse of the Self: Self-Awareness, Egotism, and the Quality of Human Life*. New York: Oxford University Press.

Leary, M. R., and R. F. Baumeister. 2000. "The Nature and Function of Self-Esteem: Sociometer Theory." *Advances in Experimental Social Psychology* 32: 1–62.

Leary, M. R., K. W. Brown, and K. J. Diebels. 2017. "Dispositional Hypo-egoicism: Insights into the Hypo-Egoic Person." In *The Oxford Handbook of Hypo-egoic Phenomena*, edited by K. W. Brown and M. R. Leary. New York: Oxford University Press.

Leary, M. R., and K. J. Diebels. 2013. "Hypo-Egoic States: What They Are, Why They Matter, and How They Occur." In *Theory Driving Research: New Wave Perspectives on Self-Processes and Human Development*, edited by M. McInerney, H. W. Marsh, R. G. Craven, and F. Guay. Charlotte, NC: Information Age.

Leary, M. R., and J. Guadagno. 2011. "The Role of Hypo-Egoic Self-Processes in Optimal Functioning and Subjective Well-Being." In *Designing Positive Psychology: Taking Stock and Moving Forward*, edited by K. M. Sheldon, T. B. Kashdan, and M. F. Steger. New York: Oxford University Press.

Lepper, M. R., and J. Henderlong. 2000. "Turning 'Play' into 'Work' and 'Work' into 'Play': 25 Years of Research on Intrinsic Versus Extrinsic Motivation." In *Intrinsic and Extrinsic Motivation: The Search for Optimal Motivation and Performance*, edited by C. Sansone and J. M. Harackiewicz. San Diego, CA: Academic Press.

Li, Y., and T. C. Bates. 2017. "Does Growth Mindset Improve Children's IQ, Educational Attainment or Response to Setbacks? Active-Control Interventions and Data on Children's Own Mindsets." Open Science Framework, July 7. https://osf.io/u5v8f/.

Linnenbrink, E. A., A. M. Ryan, and P. R. Pintrich. 1999. "The Role of Goals and Affect in Working Memory Functioning." *Learning and Individual Differences* 11 (2): 213–30.

Livingstone, S., L. Haddon, A. Görzig, and K. Ólafsson. 2011. "Risks and Safety on the Internet: The Perspective of European Children: Full Findings and Policy Implications from the EU Kids Online Survey of 9–16 Year Olds and Their Parents in 25 Countries." *EU Kids Online*, Deliverable D4. http://eprints.lse.ac.uk/id/eprint/33731.

Lumeng, J. C., P. Forrest, D. P. Appugliese, N. Kaciroti, R. F. Corwyn, and R. H. Bradley. 2010. "Weight Status As a Predictor of Being Bullied in Third Through Sixth Grades." *Pediatrics* 125 (6): e1301–7.

Marks, A. K., K. Ejesi, M. B. McCullough, and C. G. Coll. 2015. "Developmental Implications of Discrimination." In *Socioemotional Processes. Handbook of Child Psychology and Developmental Science,* vol. 3., edited by M. E. Lamb and R. M. Lerner. 7th ed. New York: John Wiley and Sons.

McDonald, K. L., M. Putallaz, C. L. Grimes, J. B. Kupersmidt, and J. D. Coie. 2007. "Girl Talk: Gossip, Friendship, and Sociometric Status." *Merrill-Palmer Quarterly* 53 (3): 381–411.

McGuire, S., B. Manke, A. Eftekhari, and J. Dunn. 2000. "Children's Perceptions of Sibling Conflict During Middle Childhood: Issues and Sibling (Dis)similarity." *Social Development* 9 (2): 173–90.

McGuire, S., S. M. McHale, and K. Updegraff. 1996. "Children's Perceptions of the Sibling Relationship in Middle Childhood: Connections Within and Between Family Relationships." *Personal Relationships* 3 (3): 229–39.

McHale, S. M., A. C. Crouter, S. McGuire, and K. A. Updegraff. 1995. "Congruence Between Mothers' and Fathers' Differential Treatment of Siblings: Links with Family Relations and Children's Well-Being." *Child Development* 66 (1): 116–28.

McLachlan, J., M. J. Zimmer-Gembeck, and L. McGregor. 2010. "Rejection Sensitivity in Childhood and Early Adolescence: Peer Rejection and Protective Effects of Parents and Friends." *Journal of Relationships Research* 1 (1): 31–40.

McLean, K. C., M. Pasupathi, and J. L. Pals. 2007. "Selves Creating Stories Creating Selves: A Process Model of Self-Development." *Personality and Social Psychology Review* 11 (3): 262–78.

Menesini, E., and C. Salmivalli. 2017. "Bullying in Schools: The State of Knowledge and Effective Interventions." *Psychology, Health and Medicine* 22 (S1): 240–53.

Meunier, J. C., I. Roskam, M. Marie Stievenart, G. Van De Moortele, D. T. Browne, and M. Wade. 2012. "Parental Differential Treatment, Child's Externalizing Behavior and Sibling Relationships: Bridging Links with Child's Perception of Favoritism and Personality, and Parents' Self-Efficacy." *Journal of Social and Personal Relationships* 29 (5): 612–38.

Meyer, W. U. 1992. "Paradoxical Effects of Praise and Criticism on Perceived Ability." *European Review of Social Psychology,* 3 (1): 259–83.

Milevsky, A. 2016. *Sibling Issues in Therapy: Research and Practice with Children, Adolescents and Adults*. New York: Palgrave Macmillan.

Mills, R. S. L. 2005. "Taking Stock of the Developmental Literature on Shame." *Developmental Review* 25 (1): 26–63.

Minuchin, S. 1974. *Families and Family Therapy*. Cambridge, MA: Harvard University Press.

Mueller, C. M. and C. S. Dweck. 1998. "Praise for Intelligence Can Undermine Children's Motivation and Performance." *Journal of Personality and Social Psychology* 75 (1): 33–52.

Neff, K. 2003. "Self-Compassion: An Alternative Conceptualization of a Healthy Attitude Toward Oneself." *Self and Identity* 2 (2): 85–101.

———. 2011. *Self-Compassion: The Proven Power of Being Kind to Yourself*. New York: HarperCollins.

Nesdale, D. 2011. "Social Groups and Children's Intergroup Prejudice: Just How Influential Are Social Group Norms?" *Anales de Psicologia*, 27 (3): 600–610.

Newman, R. S., and B. J. Murray. 2005. How Students and Teachers View the Seriousness of Peer Harassment: When Is It Appropriate to Seek Help? *Journal of Educational Psychology* 97 (3): 347–65.

Nolen-Hoeksema, S. 2001. "Gender Differences in Depression." *Current Directions in Psychological Science* 10 (5): 173–76.

Nolen-Hoeksema, S., B. E. Wisco, and S. Lyubomirsky. 2008. "Rethinking Rumination." *Perspectives on Psychological Science* 3 (5): 400–424.

Nylund, K., A. Bellmore, A. Nishina, and S. Graham. 2007. "Subtypes, Severity, and Structural Stability of Peer Victimization: What Does Latent Class Analysis Say?" *Child Development* 78 (6): 1706–22.

Olweus, D. 2012. "Cyberbullying: An Overrated Phenomenon?" *European Journal of Developmental Psychology* 9 (5): 520–38.

O'Mara, A. J., H. W. Marsh, R. G. Craven, and R. L. Debus. 2006: "Do Self-Concept Interventions Make a Difference? A Synergistic Blend of Construct Validation and Meta-Analysis." *Educational Psychologist* 41 (3): 181–206.

Orosz, G., S. Péter-Szarka, B. Böthe, I. Tóth-Király, and R. Berger. 2017. "How Not to Do a Mindset Intervention: Learning from a Mindset Intervention Among Students with Good Grades." *Frontiers in Psychology* 8 (311): 1–11.

Orth, U., and R. W. Robins. 2013. "Understanding the Link Between Low Self-Esteem and Depression." *Current Directions in Psychological Science* 22 (6): 455–60.

Orth, U., R. W. Robins, K. F. Widaman, and R. D. Conger. 2014. "Is Low Self-Esteem a Risk Factor for Depression? Findings from a Longitudinal Study of Mexican-Origin Youth." *Developmental Psychology* 50 (2): 622–33.

Paluck, E. L., and D. P. Green. 2009. "Prejudice Reduction: What Works? A Review and Assessment of Research and Practice." *Annual Review of Psychology* 60: 339–67.

Park, N. 2009. "Building Strengths of Character: Keys to Positive Youth Development." *Reclaiming Children and Youth* 18 (2): 42–47.

Park, N., and C. Peterson. 2006. "Character Strengths and Happiness Among Young Children: Content Analysis of Parental Descriptions." *Journal of Happiness Studies* 7 (3): 323–41.

———. 2008. "Positive Psychology and Character Strengths: Its Application for Strength-Based School Counseling." *Journal of Professional School Counseling* 12: 85–92.

Parkhurst, J. T., and A. Hopmeyer. 1998. "Sociometric popularity and peer-perceived popularity: Two distinct dimensions of peer status." *The Journal of Early Adolescence* 18 (2): 125–44.

Pepler, D. J., W. M. Craig, and W. L. Roberts. 1998. "Observations of Aggressive and Nonaggressive Children on the School Playground." *Merrill-Palmer Quarterly* 44 (1): 55–76.

Piff, P., P. Dietze, M. Feinberg, D. Stancato, and D. Keltner. 2015. "Awe, the Small Self, and Prosocial Behavior." *Journal of Personality and Social Psychology* 108 (6): 883–99.

Pillow, B. H. 2012. *Children's Discovery of the Active Mind*. New York: Springer.

Pomerantz, E. M., and M. M. Eaton. 2000. "Developmental Differences in Children's Conceptions of Parental Control: 'They Love Me, But They Make Me Feel Incompetent.'" *Merrill-Palmer Quarterly* 46 (1): 140–67.

Pomerantz, E. M., and S. G. Kempner. 2013. "Mothers' Daily Person and Process Praise: Implications for Children's Theory of Intelligence and Motivation." *Developmental Psychology* 49 (11): 2040–46.

Pont, S. J., R. Puhl, S. R. Cook, and W. Slusser. 2017. "Stigma Experienced by Children and Adolescents with Obesity." *Pediatrics* 140 (6): e2017303

Putallaz, M., and A. Wasserman. 1989. "Children's Naturalistic Entry Behavior and Sociometric Status: A Developmental Perspective." *Developmental Psychology* 25 (2): 297–305.

Recchia, H., C. Wainryb, and M. Pasupathi. 2013. "'Two for Flinching': Children's and Adolescents' Narrative Accounts of Harming Their Friends and Siblings." *Child Development* 84 (4): 1459–74.

Richmond, M. K., C. M. Stocker, and S. L. Rienks. 2005. "Longitudinal Associations Between Sibling Relationship Quality, Parental Differential Treatment, and Children's Adjustment." *Journal of Family Psychology* 19 (4): 550–59.

Roberts, B. W., G. Edmonds, and E. Grijalva. 2010. "It Is Developmental Me, Not Generation Me: Developmental Changes Are More Important Than Generational Changes in Narcissism—Commentary on Trzesniewski and Donnellan (2010)." *Perspectives on Psychological Science* 5 (1): 97–102.

Robins, R. W., K. H. Trzesniewski, J. L. Tracy, S. D. Gosling, and J. Potter. 2002. "Global Self-Esteem Across the Life Span." *Psychology and Aging* 17 (3): 423–34.

Rochat, P. 2003. "Five Levels of Self-Awareness As They Unfold Early in Life." *Consciousness and Cognition* 12 (4): 717–31.

Rohrer, J. M., B. Egloff, and S. C. Schmukle. 2015. "Examining the Effects of Birth Order on Personality." *Proceedings of the National Academy of Sciences of the United States of America* 112 (46): 14224–29.

Ross, H., M. Ross, N. Stein, and T. Trabasso. 2006. "How Siblings Resolve Their Conflicts: The Importance of First Offers, Planning, and Limited Opposition." *Child Development* 77 (6): 1730–45.

Rubin, K. H., R. J. Coplan, and J. C. Bowker. 2009. "Social Withdrawal in Childhood." *Annual Review of Psychology* 60: 141–71.

Rubin, K. H., R. J. Coplan, X. Chen, J. C. Bowker, K. L. McDonald, and S. Heverly-Fitt. 2015. "Peer Relationships in Childhood." *Developmental Science: An Advanced Textbook*, edited by M. H. Bornstein and M. E. Lamb. 7th ed. New York: Psychology Press.

Rubin, K. H., and L. R. Krasnor. 1986. "Social-Cognitive and Social Behavioral Perspectives on Problem Solving." In *Cognitive Perspectives on Children's Social and Behavioral Development*. The Minnesota Symposia on Child Psychology, vol. 18, edited by M. Perlmutter. Mahwah, NJ: Erlbaum.

Rutland, A., M. Killen, and D. Abrams. 2010. "A New Social-Cognitive Developmental Perspective on Prejudice: The Interplay Between Morality and Group Identity." *Perspectives on Psychological Science* 5 (3): 279–91.

Ryan, R. M., and K. W. Brown. 2003. "Why We Don't Need Self-Esteem: Basic Needs, Mindfulness, and the Authentic Self." *Psychological Inquiry* 14: 71–76.

Ryan, R. M., and E. L. Deci. 2000. "Self-Determination Theory and the Facilitation of Intrinsic Motivation, Social Development and Well-Being." *American Psychologist* 55 (1): 68–78.

Schachter, F. F., G. Gilutz, E. Shore, and M. Adler. 1978. "Sibling Deidentification Judged by Mothers: Cross-Validation and Developmental Studies." *Child Development* 49 (2): 543–46.

Schachter, F. F., E. Shore, S. Feldman-Rotman, R. E. Marquis, and S. Campbell. 1976. "Sibling Deidentification." *Developmental Psychology* 12 (5): 418–27.

Schachter, F. F., and R. K. Stone. 1987. "Comparing and Contrasting Siblings: Defining the Self." *Journal of Children in Contemporary Society* 19 (3–4): 55–75.

Scheibehenne, B., R. Greifeneder, and P. M. Todd. 2009. "What Moderates the Too-Much-Choice Effect?" *Psychology and Marketing* 26 (3): 229–53.

Schnall, S., J. Roper, and D. M. T. Fessler. 2010. "Elevation Leads to Altruistic Behavior." *Psychological Science* 21 (3): 315–20.

Scholte, R. H. J., R. C. M. E. Engels, G. Overbeek, R. A. T. de Kemp, and G. J. T. Haselager. 2007. "Stability in Bullying and Victimization and Its Association with Social Adjustment in Childhood and Adolescence." *Journal of Abnormal Child Psychology* 35 (2): 217–28.

Schonert-Reichl, K.A., E. Oberle, M. S. Lawlor, D. Abbott, K. Thomson, T. F. Oberlander, and A. Diamond. 2015. "Enhancing Cognitive and Social–Emotional Development Through a Simple-to-Administer Mindfulness-Based School Program for Elementary School Children: A Randomized Controlled Trial." *Developmental Psychology* 51 (1): 52–66.

Schwartz, D., and A. Hopmeyer Gorman. 2011. "The High Price of High Status: Popularity As a Mechanism of Risk." In *Popularity in the Peer System*, edited by A. H. N. Cillessen, D. Schwartz, and L. Mayeux. New York: Guilford Press.

Seligman, M. E. P., T. A. Steen, N. Park, and C. Peterson. 2005. "Positive Psychology Progress: Empirical Validation of Interventions." *American Psychologist* 60 (5): 410–21.

Shahar, G. 2013. "An integrative Psychotherapist's Account of His Focus When Treating Self-Critical Patients." *Psychotherapy* 50 (3): 322–25.

Shebloski, B., K. J. Conger, and K. F. Widaman. 2005. "Reciprocal Links Among Differential Parenting, Perceived Partiality, and Self-Worth: A Three-Wave Longitudinal Study." *Journal of Family Psychology* 19 (4): 633–42.

Shelley, D., and W. M. Craig. 2010. "Attributions and Coping Styles in Reducing Victimization." *Canadian Journal of School Psychology* 25 (1): 84–100.

Shiota, M., D. Keltner, and A. Mossman. 2007. "The Nature of Awe: Elicitors, Appraisals, and Effects on Self-Concept." *Cognition and Emotion* 21 (5): 944–63.

Siddiqui, A. A., and H. S. Ross. 1999. "How Do Sibling Conflicts End?" *Early Education and Development* 10 (3): 315–32.

Smith, J., and H. Ross. 2007. "Training Parents to Mediate Sibling Disputes Affects Children's Negotiation and Conflict Understanding." *Child Development* 78 (3): 790–805.

Stellar, J. E., A. Gordon, C. L. Anderson, P. K. Piff, G. D. McNeil, and D. Keltner. 2018. "Awe and humility." *Journal of Personality and Social Psychology* 114 (2): 258–69.

Stocker, C. M. 1994. "Children's Perceptions of Relationships with Siblings, Friends, and Mothers: Compensatory Processes and Links with Adjustment." *Journal of Child Psychology and Psychiatry* 35 (8): 1447–59.

Straus, M. A., R. J. Gelles, and S. K. Steinmetz. 1981. *Behind Closed Doors: Violence in the American Family.* Garden City, NY: Anchor Books.

Su, W., and A. Di Santo. 2012. "Preschool Children's Perceptions of Overweight Peers." *Journal of Early Childhood Research* 10 (1):19–31.

Swann, W. Jr., and D. Conor Seyle. 2006. "The Antecedents of Self-Esteem." In *Self-Esteem Issues and Answers,* edited by M. Kernis. New York: Psychology Press.

Tangney, J. P. 2000. "Humility: Theoretical Perspectives, Empirical Findings and Directions for Future Research." *Journal of Social and Clinical Psychology* 19 (1): 70–82.

Tangney, J. P., and R. Dearing. 2002. *Shame and Guilt.* New York: Guilford Press.

Tangney, J. P., and J. L. Tracy. 2012. Self-Conscious Emotions." In *Handbook of Self and Identity,* edited by M. Leary and J. P. Tangney. 2nd ed. New York: Guilford Press.

Tesser, A. 1980. "Self-Esteem Maintenance in Family Dynamics." *Journal of Personality and Social Psychology* 39 (1): 77–91.

Tevendale, H. D., and D. L. DuBois. 2006. "Self-Esteem Change: Addressing the Possibility of Enduring Improvements in Feelings of Self-Worth." In *Self-Esteem Issues and Answers,* edited by M. Kernis. New York: Psychology Press.

Thompson, J. A., and A. G. Halberstadt. 2008. "Children's Accounts of Sibling Jealousy and Their Implicit Theories About Relationships." *Social Development* 17 (3): 488–511.

Topper, M., P. M. Emmelkamp, E. Watkins, and T. Ehring. 2014. "Development and Assessment of Brief Versions of the Penn State Worry Questionnaire and the Ruminative Response Scale." *British Journal of Clinical Psychology* 53 (4): 402–21.

———. 2017. "Prevention of Anxiety Disorders and Depression by Targeting Excessive Worry and Rumination in Adolescents and Young Adults: A Randomized Controlled Trial." *Behaviour Research and Therapy* 90: 123–36.

Tracy, J. L., J. T. Cheng, R. W. Robins, and K. H Trzesniewski. 2009. "Authentic and Hubristic Pride: The Affective Core of Self-Esteem and Narcissism." *Self and Identity* 8 (2–3): 196–213.

Troop-Gordon, W., and L. Unhjem. 2018. "Is Preventing Peer Victimization Sufficient? The Role of Prosocial Peer Group Treatment in Children's Socioemotional Development." *Social Development*, February 2. https://doi.org/10.1111/sode.12283.

Trzesniewski, K. H., and M. B. Donnellan. 2010. "Rethinking 'Generation Me': A Study of Cohort Effects from 1976–2006." *Perspectives on Psychological Science* 5 (1): 58–75.

Trzesniewski, K. H., M. B. Donnellan, and R. W. Robins. 2003. "Stability of Self-Esteem Across the Life Span." *Journal of Personality and Social Psychology* 84 (1): 205–20.

Tucker, C. J., D. Finkelhor, A. M. Shattuck, and H. Turner. 2013. "Prevalence and Correlates of Sibling Victimization Types." *Child Abuse and Neglect* 37 (4): 213–23.

Twenge, J. M. 2013. "The Evidence for Generation Me and Against Generation We." *Emerging Adulthood* 1 (1): 11–16.

Twenge, J. M., S. Konrath, J. D. Foster, W. Keith Campbell, and B. J. Bushman. 2008. "Egos Inflating over Time: A Cross-Temporal Meta-Analysis of the Narcissistic Personality Inventory." *Journal of Personality* 76 (4): 875–902.

Underwood, M. K., and R. Faris. 2015. "#Being 13: Social Media and the Hidden World of Young Adolescents' Peer Culture." *https://assets .documentcloud.org/documents/2448422/being-13-report.pdf.*

Urquiza, A. J. and S. Timmer. 2012. "Parent-Child Interaction Therapy: Enhancing Parent-Child-Relationships." *Psychosocial Intervention* 21 (2): 145–56.

Van Cappellen, P., V. Saroglou, C. Iweins, M. Piovesana, and B. L. Fredrickson. 2013. "Self-Transcendent Positive Emotions Increase

Spirituality Through Basic World Assumptions." *Cognition and Emotion* 27 (8): 1378–94.

Vaugh, B. E., and A. J. Santos. 2009. "Structural Descriptions of Social Transactions Among Young Children: Affiliation and Dominance in Preschool Groups." In *Handbook of Peer Interactions, Relationships, and Groups*, edited by K. H. Rubin, W. M. Bukowski, and B. Laursen. New York: Guilford Press.

Verbeek, P., W. W. Hartup, and W. A. Collins. 2000. "Conflict Management in Children and Adolescents." In *Natural Conflict Resolution*, edited by F. Aureli and F. B. M. de Waal. Berkeley, CA: University of California Press.

Visconti, K. J., and W. Troop-Gordon. 2010. "Prospective Relations Between Children's Responses to Peer Victimization and Their Socioemotional Adjustment." *Journal of Applied Developmental Psychology* 31 (4): 261–72.

Volling, B. L., D. E. Kennedy, and L. M. H. Jackey. 2010. "The Development of Sibling Jealousy." In *Handbook of Jealousy: Theory, Research, and Multidisciplinary Approaches*, edited by S. L. Hart and M. Legerstee. Malden, MA: Blackwell Publishing.

Wachtel, E. 2001. "The Language of Becoming: Helping Children Change How They Think About Themselves." *Family Process* 40 (4): 369–84.

Wallace, H. M., and D. M. Tice. 2012. "Reflected Appraisal Through a 21st-Century Looking Glass." In *Handbook of Self and Identity*, edited by M. Leary and J. Tangney. 2nd ed. New York: Guilford Press.

Warneken, F., and M. Tomasello. 2008. "Extrinsic Rewards Undermine Altruistic Tendencies in 20-Month-Olds." *Developmental Psychology* 44 (6): 1785–88.

Watkins, E. R. 2016. *Rumination-Focused Cognitive-Behavioral Therapy for Depression*. New York: Guilford Press.

Watkins, E. R., and S. Nolen-Hoeksema. 2014. "A Habit-Goal Framework of Depressive Rumination." *Journal of Abnormal Psychology* 123 (1): 24–34.

Wayment, H. A., and J. J. Bauer. 2008. *Transcending Self-Interest: Psychological Explorations of the Quiet Ego*. Washington, DC: American Psychological Association.

Wayment, H. A., J. J. Bauer, and K. Sylaska. 2015. "The Quiet Ego Scale: Measuring the Compassionate Self-Identity." *Journal of Happiness Studies* 16 (4): 999–1033.

White, R. E., E. O. Prager, C. Schaefer, E. Kross, A. L. Duckworth, and S. M. Carlson. 2017. "The 'Batman Effect': Improving Perseverance in Young Children." *Child Development* 88 (5): 1563–71.

Wichmann, C., R. J. Coplan, and T. Daniels. 2004. "The Social Cognitions of Socially Withdrawn Children." *Social Development* 13 (3): 377–92.

Wigfield, A., J. S. Eccles, J. A. Fredricks, S. Simpkins, R. W. Roeser, and U. Schiefele. 2015. "Development of Achievement Motivation and Engagement." In *Socioemotional Processes*. Handbook of Child Psychology and Developmental Science, vol. 3, edited by M. E. Lamb and R. M. Lerner. 7th ed. New York: John Wiley and Sons.

Witvliet, M., P. A. Van Lier, P. Cuijpers, and H. M. Koot. 2010. "Change and Stability in Childhood Clique Membership, Isolation from Cliques, and Associated Child Characteristics." *Journal of Clinical Child and Adolescent Psychology* 39 (1): 12–24.

Wood, J. V., S. A. Heimpel, I. R. Newby-Clark, and M. Ross. 2005. "Snatching Defeat from the Jaws of Victory: Self-Esteem Differences in the Experience and Anticipation of Success." *Journal of Personality and Social Psychology* 89 (5): 764–80.

Wood, J. V., W. Q. E. Perunovic, and J. W. Lee. 2009. "Positive Self-Statements: Power for Some, Peril for Others." *Psychological Science* 20 (7): 860–66.

Zenner, C., S. Herrnleben-Kurz, and H. Walach. 2014. "Mindfulness-Based Interventions in Schools—A Systematic Review and Meta-analysis." *Frontiers in Psychology* 5: 603.

Eileen Kennedy-Moore, PhD, is a clinical psychologist based in Princeton, NJ, and mom of four. A trusted expert on children's feelings and friendships, Kennedy-Moore is a professor for *The Great Courses*, serves on the advisory board for *Parents* magazine, and blogs for *Psychology Today*.

Kennedy-Moore has written or coauthored many books, including *Growing Friendships: A Kids' Guide to Making and Keeping Friends*, *Smart Parenting for Smart Kids*, *The Unwritten Rules of Friendship*, *What's My Child Thinking?*, and *What About Me? Twelve Ways to Get Your Parents' Attention (Without Hitting Your Sister)*. Her audio-video series is called *Raising Emotionally and Socially Healthy Kids*.

Learn more at www.eileenkennedymoore.com, www.drfriendtastic.com, and www.growingfriendshipsblog.com.

Foreword writer **Michele Borba, EdD**, is an educational psychologist and internationally recognized parenting and character development expert. She is the author of twenty-four books, including her latest, *UnSelfie: Why Empathetic Kids Succeed in Our All-About-Me World*.

MORE BOOKS *from*
NEW HARBINGER PUBLICATIONS

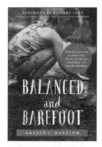

Register your **new harbinger** titles for additional benefits!

When you register your **new harbinger** title—purchased in any format, from any source—you get access to benefits like the following:

- Downloadable accessories like printable worksheets and extra content

- Instructional videos and audio files

- Information about updates, corrections, and new editions

Not every title has accessories, but we're adding new material all the time.

Access free accessories in 3 easy steps:

1. Sign in at NewHarbinger.com (or **register** to create an account).

2. Click on **register a book**. Search for your title and click the **register** button when it appears.

3. Click on the **book cover or title** to go to its details page. Click on **accessories** to view and access files.

That's all there is to it!

If you need help, visit:

NewHarbinger.com/accessories

new harbinger
CELEBRATING
40 YEARS